# HOW TO SET UP AND MANAGE A CORPORATE LEARNING CENTRE

# How to set up and manage a corporate learning centre

Samuel A. Malone

Gower

Published by
Gower Publishing Limited
Gower House
Croft Road
Aldershot
Hampshire GU11 3HR
England

Gower
Old Post Road
Brookfield
Vermont 05036
USA

Reprinted 1997

Samuel A Malone has asserted his right under the Copyright, Designs and Patents Act 1988 to be identified as the author of this work.

Gower Publishing would like to thank International Organizational Leadership Ltd, Dublin, Ireland and M4 Business Training, Corsham, Wiltshire, UK, for their help in publishing this book.

British Library Cataloguing in Publication Data
Malone, S. A.
   How to set up and manage a corporate learning centre
   1. Continuing education centres 2. Continuing education
   3. Employees – Training of
   I. Title
   658.3'124'3

ISBN 0 566 07818 X

Library of Congress Cataloging-in-Publication Data
Malone, Samuel A.
   How to set up and manage a corporate learning centre / Samuel A. Malone
      p.   cm.
   ISBN 0–566–07818–X (cloth)
   1. Organizational learning—Technological innovations. 2. Open
learning—Management. 3. Information technology—Management.
4. Employees—Training of—Technological innovations. I. Title.
HD58.82.M35   1997
658.3'12404—dc20                                        96–15514
                                                            CIP

Typeset in 11 point Palatino by Bournemouth Colour Press, Parkstone, Poole, Dorset and printed in Great Britain at the University Press, Cambridge.

# Contents

# Figures

# Preface

The knowledge acquired in university degrees and professional qualifications becomes out of date within a few years. People now change their careers several times during a lifetime. The concept of a job for life is a thing of the past. To survive and progress in the modern workplace you must continually update your knowledge and skills. You must adopt the idea of continuous personal development and lifelong learning to survive in a rapidly changing world.

The modern workplace must become like a university, continually developing and learning, if companies are to maintain their competitive edge. The information age has arrived. Information is power. Information is the most valuable and marketable product in the world. Information provides added value and differentiates one company from another. With competitive products becoming very similar companies are differentiating by service and knowledge. Welcome to the information age.

This book will show you how to make education, training, knowledge and skill accessible to everybody in the workplace irrespective of their formal education through the use of modern information technology. Soon the PC will be as commonplace in the home as the television set is today. So every home will have the equivalent of a corporate learning centre.

The nucleus of a corporate learning centre is already in the home with television, video recorders, the telephone and the PC. The telecommunications technology with cablelink and so on is already with us. In the past few years there has been an explosion in the range and quality of educational software programmes available on audio, video, CBT and CD-ROM. It is now possible to bring advanced education and training programmes into your own living room. Knowledge is no longer the preserve of scholars in cloistered universities. It is accessible on your PC and TV screen. The democratization of education is coming. The barriers to education are falling down. Progressive institutions such as the Open University are exploiting modern technology to make university education accessible to those who otherwise could not use it.

Corporate learning centres now supplement live training and on-the-job training in many large companies. This book will show you how to set up and manage a corporate learning centre in your company. It will discuss the motives behind the organizational issues involved in setting up a corporate learning centre and alert you to the type of resistances that may be encountered. The management, marketing and administration of a corporate learning centre is discussed in some detail.

S. A. Malone, M.Ed MIIE FIITD ACMA ACIS

# 1 Introduction and definitions

## The need for open learning

Until the arrival of open, distance and flexible learning many people were prevented from furthering their education or improving their vocational skills and qualifications. In particular, those with jobs and families were not catered for by conventional third-level education with its constraints of time, prescription, space and cost. Even with adult education classes you have to attend at a particular time and place and follow regulations designed more for the convenience of the administrators and educators rather than for meeting the needs of the adult learner. Most of these courses require formal educational qualifications on entry. Attending courses in outside training establishments, in many cases, presents the same kinds of problems. People in rural areas find that training opportunities are almost non-existent. It is only in the large urban centres that you find a broad range of training programmes. This rigidity of timetabling, location and administration can defeat all except the most determined.

The providers of education have been slow to adopt the marketing concept, i.e. find out exactly what the customer wants and then provide the service or product to satisfy that want. The customers in this context are the students and parents of students. Parent/Teacher councils are a step in the right direction. With the arrival of the Open University and the distance learning degrees of many prestigious universities this gap in the market is now being filled in the formal educational area.

The advent of new technology such as computer-based training (CBT), interactive video (IV), video and audio, electronic mail (e-mail) and video conferencing now means that it has become feasible for many organizations to bring open learning into the workplace. It is possible to provide training economically on most topics to small groups. Employees were often precluded from training and development opportunities because of lack of variety, flexibility, availability and accessibility of courses. Now training to meet specific needs can be brought right to their doorstep and used as and when required.

## Purpose and layout of book

The purpose of this book is to provide you with the necessary information to set up and manage your own corporate learning centre. Chapter 1, as well as giving a brief overview of the book, defines open, distance and flexible learning and shows how the three are incorporated into the concept of corporate learning centres. Open learning courses make learning accessible, easy, interactive, self-paced and interesting and thus combine aspects of open, distance and flexible learning

Chapter 2 looks at some of the reasons why a company should establish a corporate learning centre. The key benefits of open learning, including accessibility, flexibility, modular structure and continuous feedback, are examined in some detail.

Chapter 3 considers making the most of a corporate learning centre. The importance of identifying training needs, of a good syllabus and the need to evaluate training are addressed. Some successful corporate learning centres are considered.

Chapter 4 examines the need to establish costs and measure benefits. It also looks at the costs and savings made by various companies who have successfully established corporate learning centres

Chapter 5 explores the resistances to open learning from managers, trainers and learners and how to resolve them. The force field model is used to help analyse the factors which help and hinder open learning.

In Chapter 6 the problems and challenges of launching a corporate learning centre are examined. The layout of a typical centre including the organization of learning booths is also discussed.

Chapter 7 discusses the media used in corporate learning centres. These include CBT, IV, CD-ROM, CDI, audio, video, the Internet and e-mail, text-based courses and magazines and journals. Their strengths and weaknesses are considered.

Chapter 8 looks at the management and administration of a corporate learning centre. A person specification and a job specification for the coordinator is considered as well as the coordinator's role and tasks.

Chapter 9 shows you how to market a corporate learning centre. It considers the mission statement, the centre's objective, marketing strategies, objectives and plans and the need to link these with strategic plans.

Chapter 10 is a learner's guide to using a corporate learning centre. It includes scheduling visits, setting personal objectives, choosing courses, recording progress and keeping your manager and coordinator informed about your plans and progress.

Finally, Chapter 11 draws some conclusions and makes some recommendations for the success of corporate learning centres.

Appendix 1 is a case study concerning the setting up of a corporate learning centre at Sun Life. The launch of the centre, benefits of open learning and the introduction of CD-ROM are considered.

## Introduction to distance, flexible and open learning

What is distance learning? What is flexible learning? What is open learning? Do they mean exactly the same or are they three different concepts? The following sections will examine the issues.

### *Distance learning*

Distance learning takes place at a distance from the preparer and presenter of the learning material. The material is of a high quality and is produced with the end user in mind. Correspondence courses were the original distance learning programmes. They were essentially text-based and were widely used by the accountancy and other business professions.

For nearly 100 years correspondence colleges have been preparing accountancy students to qualify as professional members of the various accountancy bodies and other business institutes such as Chartered Secretaries and Personnel Management. These colleges gave people the opportunity to qualify as professionals by self-study without attending educational establishments.

The institutes set examinations and standards but do not concern themselves with the mode of preparation. This process is left to the discretion of the student and is very flexible. Thus many trainee accountants, who work during the day and spend many nights away from the home base on audit assignments, study accountancy through a correspondence course in their own time but often with the financial support of the employer. Handy (1988) sees this approach to corporate learning as the way forward in the future:

> The kind of management training system that I see is one modelled on our professions like accountancy. Every would be manager, be he or she engineer, chemist, computer expert or whatever, should have done some homework and learned the language of his or her profession before he or she is more than two or three years in the job. That can be readily and easily done through that delivery system that we are so great at: open learning supported by company-based mentors.

The Japanese use the correspondence course as a cost-effective method to upgrade executive skills in business and management theory. As Handy points out: 'Self-enlightenment is Japanese for correspondence courses'.

The text in correspondence school courses these days has been, in many cases, supplemented by audio, video, CBT, CD-ROM, IV and, of course, books. Distance learning, unlike correspondence courses, is now usually supported by residential courses which give learners the opportunity to meet others and tutors, guidance in workshops and on the telephone.

In response to market demand, distance learning has now been adopted by many universities. The leader in this field is, of course, the Open University. Adult learners may now acquire certificate, diploma, primary degrees, masters degrees and up to PhD level through this medium. Freathy (1991), for example, describes a distance learning MBA in retailing and wholesaling run by Stirling University. Johnston (1993) says that evidence from Sheffield University's distance learning masters degree in training and development suggests a high level of satisfaction with this method of continuing professional development from participants and sponsoring companies. Busy professionals are given the opportunity to obtain a masters degree while continuing to work.

Distance learning can be integrated with the facilities and programmes of the corporate learning centres, which means that employees on distance learning programmes can use the courseware of the corporate learning centres to help them in their studies as well as in their jobs. Some professional bodies, such as the Institute of Bankers and the accountancy institutes, have produced complete subject programmes for their examinations using the CBT media that is available in corporate learning centres. Corporate learning centres can be linked up to educational establishments in order to obtain certification or national vocational qualifications for their courses.

Birchall (1990) introduces the idea of third generation distance learning. He says the approach adopted in the early 1980s may be considered second generation distance learning, first generation being traditional correspondence education. Students use various media – mostly audio, video, CBT and text-based. In addition, they are offered 'support services' comprising helpline and tutor-led workshops. This type of service could be provided by corporate learning centres.

Third generation distance learning aims to overcome the lack of interaction and problems of isolation experienced by many distance learners. It gives the student access to others from the workplace or home. Video-conferencing and e-mail are being used for remote teaching. E-mail can be used both for transmission of information direct to the home and also for conferencing. Both facilities offer scope for two-way communication and give a new dimension to education. Voice mail means that the tutor can offer guidance and advice even when the student is not at home.

## *Flexible learning*

Flexible learning is a term used to describe both open and distance learning. In practice the three terms open, distance and flexible learning are often used interchangeably but in theory, as indicated, there may be subtle differences between them. Van den Brande (1993) defines flexible learning as follows:

> Flexible learning is enabling learners to learn when they want (frequency, timing, duration), how they want (modes of learning), and what they want (that is learners can define what constitutes learning to them). These flexible learning principles may be applied at a distance. If so then the term 'distance learning' is used. In such cases the learners can choose where they want to learn (at home, at an institution or company, at a training centre, etc.).

In addition, throughout the world, open, distance and flexible learning are defined differently. This is not merely the result of different languages and culture, but rather the outcome of different educational, training and vocational training systems and alternative applications of new technology. Thus the term 'Fernunterricht' (distance education) is used in Germany, 'open learning' in the UK and 'formation multimedia' in France.

## *Open learning*

Open learning suggests that there are no prequalifications necessary to do the programme such as age, status or formal examinations. It also suggests flexibility in where to learn – such as at home; when to learn – such as in the morning, at lunchtime or in the evening; how to learn – the delivery system such as text, CBT, CD-ROM, IV, audio and video; and the pace at which to learn which is decided by the adult learner. In practice many 'open learning' programmes run by educational or training establishments may set minimum academic standards and other criteria for admission.

A corporate learning centre is just one application of the concept of open learning and is the one we are principally concerned with in this book. Other applications would be correspondence schools and, of course, the Open University. In a corporate learning centre learning is made accessible to all staff who want to learn and go on learning. It's a type of industrial democracy in action providing learner empowerment. The emphasis is on continuous learning and improvement throughout an employee's career.

Corporate learning centre courses make learning accessible, easy, self-paced and interesting. The courses are designed around different forms of media. They range from text-based, audio and video tapes to CBT, CD-ROM, IV and e-mail. However, unlike teacher-centred conventional learning, the responsibility for open learning is on the learner. Knowledge is power and the medium of open learning is a type of real learner empowerment. We are fast becoming a knowledge-based society.

In this book the term 'corporate learning centre' combines aspects of the three ideas of open, distance and flexible learning (see Figure 1.1).

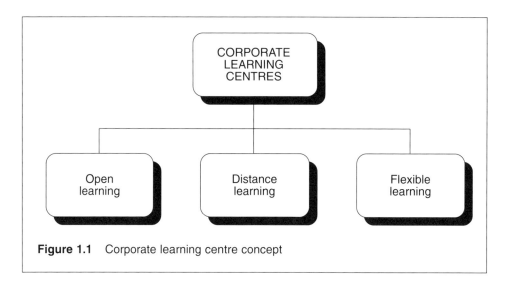

**Figure 1.1**　Corporate learning centre concept

Corporate learning centres are open because employees may avail themselves of their services without regard to grade, gender, age, disability, qualifications and so on. In addition, staff studying the distance learning programmes of the main universities and professional bodies may use the facilities of the corporate learning centres to prepare themselves for examinations. In fact, complete subject areas are now available on CBT and there is a vast number of topical academic areas on audio and video.

For example, the BBC, Open University, Melrose, Fenman and Gower among others have shown what can be done by producing high quality audio and video programmes aimed at third level and professional students. These videos may be purchased and used in corporate learning centres. Where an organization is geographically scattered through a branch network the services of the centre may be accessed through wide area networks (WAN). Corporate learning centres offer flexibility in that learners may learn when they want, how they want and what they want.

## Traditional versus corporate learning centre training

Traditional training is done in groups and to a fixed schedule. The style and pace of delivery is influenced by the group. There is fear of exposure on the part of the trainee. The training tends to be interactive but specific to the training needs of the trainees. On the other hand, corporate learning centre training is taken individually (although pairs is sometimes recommended) and delivery is flexible in that you can skip ahead or move back and repeat if necessary. The pace of delivery is determined by the user. The corporate learning centre is managed by a generalist coordinator and the learning environment is seen as non-threatening. There is limited interaction and programmes are generic in nature in that they are designed for mass audiences. A summary comparison is shown in Figure 1.2.

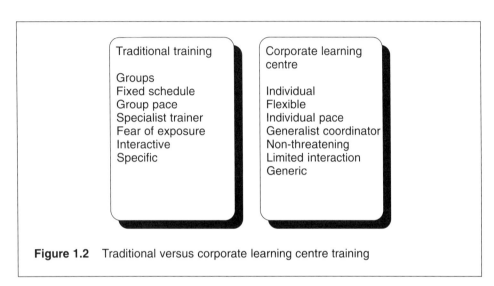

**Figure 1.2**   Traditional versus corporate learning centre training

## Summary

Distance learning takes place at a distance from the preparer and presenter of the learning material. Correspondence courses were the original distance learning programmes. Flexible learning is a term used to describe both open and distance learning. Flexible learning enables people to learn when they want, where they want and what they want.

Open learning suggests that there are no prequalifications necessary to do the programmes, such as age, status or formal examinations. A corporate learning centre is just one application of the concept of open learning. Corporate learning centre courses make learning accessible, easy, self-paced and interesting. They combine aspects of the three ideas of open learning, distance and flexible learning.

# 2    Why establish a corporate learning centre?

## Introduction

Corporate learning centres are designed to:

- increase productivity and cost-effectiveness by improving employees' on-the-job performance and their ability to cope with change, developments in technology or equip them to take on extra responsibility
- create a learning culture throughout the organization.

The success of the centre will be reflected in improved job satisfaction, increased morale, greater efficiency, improved customer service, increased quality, reduced costs and greater profits.

Knowledge-based added value is the key competitive advantage of any company. Most studies suggest that properly managed open learning is more cost effective than traditional methods of training and enables employees to learn faster and retain more. This is particularly true where large numbers need to be trained in standardized procedures or small numbers in dangerous procedures or in the use of expensive equipment.

The motives for introducing corporate learning centres include a desire to keep up to date with information technology, facilitating the learning organization ethos and making provision for continuing professional education. The key benefits of open learning are that it recognizes the fact that different people learn at different speeds and in different ways; it is an active form of learning; it helps individuals accept responsibility for their own learning, it helps people to learn how to learn; it generates motivation and dispels the idea that attendance at courses is the equivalent of effort and achievement. In addition, rising standards of computer literacy, the increased sophistication of PC technology, improved telecommunications systems, the greater variety of software available and falling costs in both software and hardware have all helped the process along.

## Information technology revolution

In the last few years there has been a gradual move away from total reliance on a tutor-centred approach to a more student-centred and self-reliant approach. Organizationally there has been a move away from central control of training to decentralization and learner empowerment. In a competitive situation, with a need to reduce costs, training and development is often seen as a non-core activity. Thus there are always pressures on management to reduce the training budget or get more value from the training investment. Consequently, in times of recession training is often the first business activity to be cut back. Decentralization of training and cuts in training costs can now be achieved with the application of computer-based technology. In addition, a company may feel that it has fallen behind in the rapidly changing information technology scene. As a result it may need to bring a large number of its staff up to date in the latest information technology quickly and cost effectively.

The logistics of providing live courses in information technology, or indeed any subject, to large numbers of employees is formidable and expensive. This could be substantially met by encouraging staff to do it themselves more cost effectively in corporate learning centres. In fact, corporate learning centres are particularly suited for information technology skills and the quality and range of CD-ROM courses now available in this area is impressive.

Computer literacy skills are now as important in business as the more conventional skills of reading, writing and arithmetic. Familiarity with computerized corporate systems and the better known desktop publishing, word processing, spreadsheet and graphics software packages are now considered essential for many jobs. In the new information age everybody should have some familiarity with computers.

The use of different media in the corporate learning centre will also develop new competencies in staff through familiarization with audio, video, CBT, CD-ROM, IV and e-mail and the hands-on approach to computer hardware. People's fears about using computers are quickly overcome. In any event the helpful tutorial skills and friendly guidance of the learning centre coordinator are always on hand when needed. More importantly, the corporate learning centre gives people a resource that they can use to help solve work-related problems.

# Learning organization

Most organizations want to be seen as modern, progressive and go ahead. Corporate learning centres are a relatively new and cost-effective approach to the delivery of training. If you want to maintain your competitive advantage you need to keep up with improvements in information technology. What is more important is that your staff must have the expertise to use the information technology effectively. This expertise can now be self taught in corporate learning centres. Firms also want to be seen to be doing something concrete to demonstrate their commitment to become a learning organization and support the concept of lifelong continuous learning and learner empowerment.

Many experts claim that the Japanese maintain their competitive edge through their considerable investment in training. Surveys show that Britain and Ireland fall badly behind in investment in training compared with other EU countries, such as Germany which is renowned for its training culture, the USA and Japan. Open learning is now seen as a practical, cost effective and democratic method to train, educate, develop and empower staff and an efficient way to bridge the training gap.

In the West we must move away from Taylor's scientific management approach that the boss knows best and has a monopoly on knowledge. Under this approach the planning and control of work is seen as the manager's responsibility. The manager designs the work methods and workers are meant to do what they are told. It is the conventional command and control approach. Thus workers are seen as brawn rather than brain. Modern management thinking now suggests workers should have a say in work design. Therefore, we must encourage employees to use their intelligence and creativity to improve work methods and processes and to become more self-reliant.

With its use of modern technology the corporate learning centre exposes staff to the latest developments in information technology. Keyboarding and PC familiarization programmes are available for the novice to help them get started. For the more advanced learner there are CD-ROM courses available on all the leading software packages including windows. People using the CD-ROM-based courses find them in many cases as good as, if not better than, the equivalent live courses and much more flexible and cost effective. The CD-ROM-based courses have the added advantage of self-pacing with the facility of repeated practice as required.

# Open learning underpins the knowledge-based society

Corporate learning centres, through the application of educational technology, use a different delivery system to meet training and development needs. Open learning should be seen as complementary to, rather than a substitute for, conventional training. Waterhouse (1990) suggests that it equips people for the demands of working life in a rapidly changing, highly technological society. Computer-based training is now capable of delivering a wide variety of quality training programmes which a well staffed conventional training department could not match. It has been estimated that the knowledge base of society is now doubling every seven years. In the modern world most people will change jobs and pursue different careers during a lifetime. It's therefore essential that you are willing to upgrade your existing skills and able to learn new skills as necessary. The most important life skills are now considered to be learning to learn skills and the ability to go on learning.

## Continuing professional education

A number of professional bodies, including accounting, engineering and personnel institutes, now require their members to upgrade their skills each year. In the modern rapidly changing world knowledge and skills quickly become out of date. Engineers, accountants, technicians now realize that their knowledge base quickly becomes obsolete unless they take positive action to keep up to date. Professional knowledge is likely to be out of date within five years unless updated.

Professions recognize the need for lifelong learning. Some of the programmes stocked in the corporate learning centre should meet the requirements of the institutes continuing professional education. This saves on the cost of employee attendance at outside courses which can be quite expensive for companies to support. The certification of corporate learning centre courses can be arranged with local educational institutes.

## Key benefits of open learning

Harper (1993) summarizes the case for open learning from the learner's perspective as follows:

- recognises that different students learn at different speeds and in different ways;
- helps students to be more active in their learning;
- helps students to accept greater responsibility for their own learning;
- helps students to learn how to learn;
- generates motivation and commitment and stimulates a sense of self-management;
- dispels the student idea that attendance in class is equivalent to effort and achievement.

### People learn at different speeds and in different ways

In a 'live' training course the trainer's presentation is aimed at a common denominator of participants' experience, knowledge and ability, so that individual variations in learning ability are not catered for. Repetition and practice is a key principle of learning and one that open learning courses facilitate. Trainees can go back over different areas as often as necessary until the relevant skill or knowledge base is acquired. In 'live' training this is not practicable. Using computer courseware you can be sure that the same standard programme is provided for each trainee, whereas in live training variations will occur due to changes in delivery and mood and the receptiveness of the learner.

Computer-based training (CBT) caters for different learning styles. Research into how people learn and remember suggests that we retain about 20 per cent of what we hear, 40 per cent of what we see and hear, and 75 per cent of what we see, hear, and do. Multimedia engages all the senses – hearing, seeing and doing – and thus maximizes learning while catering for every learning style.

Comparative studies suggest that learning effectiveness of CBT is superior to conventional training – people learn faster and retain more – some studies showing an improvement in the time required to learn of 50 per cent. This is due to:

- self-pacing – because the learning is self-paced the learner can take the most efficient path to learn the content
- interaction and feedback – the courseware is specially designed to provide reinforcement by giving plenty of practice. In some courses learners are not allowed to progress until earlier stages have been mastered.

## More focused and active learning

In a corporate learning centre course people can focus on exactly the area they want to develop. Peripheral areas can be ignored. They can concentrate on the issues that are currently relevant to their needs. They can move back, fast forward, skip, stop, repeat and exit as they please.

With the rapid advances in information technology the shortcomings of programmed learning on cumbersome teaching machines has been largely overcome. In fact, the best of learning theory has now been successfully incorporated into the design of CBT programmes to help people learn enjoyably, quickly and effectively. Fricker (1988) maintains that open learning courses should be user friendly, the content and style should be practical and visually good and facilitate active learning.

## Learner responsibility

Open learning develops self-reliance and initiative. Temple (1988) maintains that enterprising, self-starting and self-directing people are what companies need. In a fast changing and competitive environment companies need to develop staff with self-reliance and initiative and who are keen to learn and equip themselves with new skills. The philosophy that managers have a monopoly on brainpower, ideas and knowledge is going. The creativity and knowledge of the workforce must be engaged. The development of intellectual capital must be encouraged and nurtured.

Open learning is an ideal means of developing the necessary skills and attitudes of self-reliance and initiative precisely because they are exactly those which are acquired when doing open learning. Staff who are self-reliant do not wait around to be told what to learn. They identify their own training needs and then set about meeting those needs themselves. Open learning provides the facilities to do this. In practice, some people may not be self-motivated, self-disciplined and capable of taking responsibility for their own learning. These people need the traditional training approach with a trainer for encouragement and direction. They also need the encouragement and guidance of managers to undertake training.

## Helps learners how to learn

A feature of CBT is the interaction and continuous feedback and evaluation of performance. The principles of programmed learning are used in the design of courses. The whole emphasis of CBT is on facilitating learners to learn effectively. Information is presented in chunks with associated questions to test understanding – the stimulus, response, reinforcement principle. Learners do not move ahead until the relevant skill or knowledge has been mastered. There is a gradual acquisition of skill and expertise with little chance of information overload. Because of the proximity of the workplace staff can immediately apply the skills and knowledge learned in the real work situation.

Feedback is an important principle in learning and is automatically built in to well-designed quality open learning courses. Some do not allow you to progress until you have satisfactorily dealt with the previous section. More formal assessment may also be a feature of open learning programmes. These could take the form of examinations, questionnaires or progress tests.

## Motivation

The availability of a corporate learning centre in a company is a great boost to staff morale and motivation. It is a visible demonstration that the company cares about the development of its employees. Learners are made autonomous and can identify and meet their own training needs as and when required. They set their own learning objectives and become responsible for their own learning and thus feel a sense of empowerment. As Coldeway (1982) points out, this is in line with modern educational theory and management thinking.

To attract learners the training experience provided by the corporate learning centre must give employees an opportunity to develop competencies directly relevant to their jobs. The training must be perceived as useful for career progression and promotion inside or outside the company. Using the corporate learning centre must have status and acceptability with the employees' peer group. These factors will affect the motivation of learners.

## Attendance does not mean effort and achievement

Attendance at a live course does not mean that people are actually learning. Individuals may be nominated by their managers to attend training courses sometimes against the wishes of the attendee. In such circumstances they will have little commitment to the training. Other people are sent on courses for the wrong reasons, i.e. as reward for good on-the-job performance or for rest and recreation. Such individuals are also unlikely to be committed to the training. In any case, it is easier to daydream and lose concentration in a live training situation than when doing a corporate learning centre course, because of the more frequent interaction and feedback involved in open learning courseware.

## Accessibility of time and place

Barriers to traditional training often exist because of lack of accessibility. This may be due to lack of availability of courses, distance, domestic and work-related constraints. Corporate learning centres bring training directly to the user at a convenient time and place, using top quality and proven course material.

## Flexibility

Staff can study open learning courses at their own pace, in their own time and without supervision, threat or fear of competition. Lunch time, before or after normal working hours, weekends and any time during work allowed by their managers may be suitable. Shift workers, because of their unsociable hours, can make use of learning opportunities that would not normally be available to them. Courses can be studied and complicated topics repeated as necessary.

Training is provided all year round, on demand, which is not possible in a live training situation. In addition many educational and training establishments close down for summer, Christmas and Easter vacations. Disruption of work is minimized, travelling time and accommodation costs are eliminated. People become more flexible in their attitudes to new methods and new technology especially to the acceptance of change through continuous lifelong learning. The 'drop in and help yourself to learning' attitude creates an ethos and culture of learning in the individual and in the organization. The barriers to learning are eliminated when it becomes available to all employees.

One of the big advantages of a corporate learning centre is that staff with some spare time can make use of the opportunity there and then to upgrade their knowledge and skills instead of wasting time attending an internal or external 'live' course at a set time which may not suit them.

## *Equality*

There are many reasons why staff do not take up training and development opportunities. Some women, but also men, find it difficult to attend courses held centrally in headquarters, entailing travel and being away overnight, because of family commitments. Part-time workers, temporary staff and job sharers are often excluded from traditional training and development courses. The courses in a corporate learning centre are more accessible. Open learning is seen as a means of meeting their needs without disruption of work, travelling time and overnight stays.

Research studies show that older people tend to learn more slowly than younger ones and that there is a small decline in their working memory. Older staff are often reluctant to go on 'live' training programmes because of fear of not being able to keep up and looking foolish in front of their younger colleagues. The privacy and self-pacing of the corporate learning centre approach overcomes this problem. Older learners find computer-based training to be of special advantage because they are able to control the pace of their work, the amount of revision of difficult issues, and the ways in which they can explore and test out new concepts. A corporate learning centre will provide the facilities for lifelong learning, irrespective of age, and opportunities for personal development and possible career advancement.

It is good company policy that learning opportunities on a democratic basis should be provided for a greater range and number of employees. The corporate learning centre provides this opportunity and puts the onus for learning on the learner – where it should be. The learner's requirement is the commitment to learn expressed in the form of time, willpower, persistence, dedication and application. Learning is hard work. It requires pain and sacrifice in the present for future gain.

## Maintaining competitive advantage

Specific training needs should be integrated into individual training plans and work programmes derived from annual business plans and the strategic objective. The idea of continuous improvement is essential if a business is to prosper and survive. Continuous improvements in product design, manufacturing process, customer service, organization structure, information technology and telecommunications mean that employees must frequently update their knowledge and skills. The modern workplace needs to become more and more like the learning community of a university. Corporate learning centres should be a visible underpinning of the philosophy of the learning organization and the concept of lifelong learning, training and development.

## Modular basis

Corporate learning centre courses are organized on a modular basis. Remember that the length of a module should be reasonably short in order not to demotivate people. A journey of 1,000 miles begins with a single step. People are motivated to learn by concentrating on objectives which are supported by achievable and manageable 'chunks' of material. Reinforcement and reward should be a feature of each step.

The modular design of courses also facilitates use as and when staff have the available time, which in practice may be in half-hour blocks. In fact, since the average attention span is about 20 minutes, half-hour study sessions are about the ideal length to maximize concentration and learning. To maintain concentration learners should be advised to take five-minute breaks every hour and two-minute breaks every 20 minutes. Open learning not only gives the learner power to define when and over what period they might learn and when to take breaks, but also the content and form of the learning.

With the modular structure of most courseware learners can use the menu to go to the particular topic that they want. Thus there is no need to go through information that you know already and learning is speeded up.

Miller, a psychologist, discovered the 7 plus or minus 2 rule of memory which suggests that people have difficulty learning more than nine items at a time. Modular design on this basis would suggest that courseware should contain not more than 9 modules, each with not more than 9 sections and each section containing not more than 9 points. This is important to keep in mind when designing or selecting courseware. The modular design enables people to move around the programme quickly without having to stick to a rigid sequence. A good menu will facilitate the process.

## Greater quality control

The quality and relevance of open learning courseware can be tested and judged in advance. Consistency of presentation, which is not possible with traditional training, is assured. Deciding whether to send somebody on an external course is often determined by a glossy brochure rather than proper validation.

The quality of course materials used in open learning will be consistent and not subject to a trainer's 'off day'. Trainers are released from routine training and can concentrate on the more demanding, urgent and specific needs of their organization. The standard of courseware has improved considerably over the years and the range and quality of software programmes is good. Choose the best material available for your corporate learning centre.

Most programmes are now designed in line with the best educational and learning principles. Open learning courseware is piloted extensively before launch by the vendors. Feedback is collected from a sample of learners via questionnaires, interviews and so on. Modifications are based on the feedback obtained. Because of the known costs, budgets should be easier to compile, control and manage.

## Simulating safety procedures

Multimedia courseware enables employees to explore safely the operation of expensive and potentially dangerous equipment in a risk-free environment. On-the-job safety routines can also be learnt, such as power station operation simulators for the training of power workers and flight simulators for training pilots. Lavitt (1995), for example, reports than an Israeli company is offering a multimedia Aircraft Recognition Training (ART) system that can be used for all phases of training pilots, aircrews and intelligence personnel. The sophistication of simulators has been enhanced with the development of virtual reality and the potential applications of this new technology is enormous.

Safety, health and welfare programmes are now available on video, CD-ROM and IV. Some companies produce their own videos which deal specifically with their country's legislation and specific organizational requirements on this subject. Remember there is a statutory requirement that a company complies with safety legislation and that employees receive proper instruction in safety procedures.

## Job aids

Job aids can provide just-in-time training. They may be programmed into the computer as a form of on-the-job training to be used as and when required. Many skills are learned and retained better when there is an immediate need to learn them. Job aids can be used instead of cumbersome procedural manuals, detailed work guides or looking for assistance from your supervisor. Ganger (1994) reports that in a typical bank job aid system, employees use a desktop computer when a customer requests any of a dozen relatively complicated bank services. The employee enters the type of transaction and the job aid programme produces a listing of all forms needed, where to locate them and the procedures that must be performed. Obviously, with the passage of time the user will become less reliant on the system to identify forms and procedures and will become self-sufficient.

## No panacea for all training needs

Open learning is unlikely to be a panacea for all training needs. Computer-based training is very appropriate for technical topics such as accountancy, information technology and engineering. A significant number of training departments now use CBT to teach computer-related as well as other technical skills. However, some areas such as the soft skills are better dealt with by other methods including traditional educational and training courses and on-the-job training.

For example, you could learn all about the theory of driving a car from watching a video or doing a computer-based course, but you would still be unable to drive the car. You need practical competencies which can only be acquired by driving.

For business and management subjects you can pick up the theory from CBT programmes but this needs to be supported by on-the-job experience if you want to acquire real understanding and practical expertise. The theory of public speaking can be learned in a corporate learning centre course, but the practical skills can only be acquired in a 'live' programme. Similarly, you could learn all about the theory of writing by working through a computer-based programme but you still need practice and live coaching in writing skills.

Kattackal (1994) reports that:

> CBT represents only one piece of the training puzzle. It should not be chosen in isolation, but rather it should be linked to other training efforts, including on-the-job training. A new staff member can learn about the audit process by having the computer present audit concepts, methods, and techniques via CBT. However, this type of training in isolation will not produce a competent auditor.
>
> The development of presentation and writing skills, interviewing techniques, and analytical skills are just some of the complex topics that cannot be readily taught using a software program ... at least, not yet. In general, CBT is a clear choice for learning software applications; but, so far, it's not particularly effective at imparting audit skills.

Stephenson (1992) found that even with CBT the presence of a tutor improves performance: 'There is simply something about having another human around and aware of your actions that alters your behaviour'.

There is a danger that a corporate learning centre may be seen as good in itself rather than its effects. The technology looks good and impressive and may be seen as an end in itself rather than just another way of delivering training. In fact, in some companies corporate learning centres have not been successful and have been closed down largely due to inadequate planning, poor marketing and lack of management and employee support. A corporate learning centre offers a cost-effective alternative to some traditional forms of training. If this is unlikely to be the case in your organization, then don't make the investment.

## Summary

In the last few years there has been a gradual move away from total reliance on a tutor-centred approach to a more student-centred and self-reliant approach. Rising standards of computer literacy, the increased sophistication of PC technology, improved telecommunications systems, the greater variety of software available and falling costs of hardware and software have all helped this process along. The need to empower employees and to create a learning organization culture have been other motivators for corporate learning centres.

The key benefits of open learning are:

- caters for people who learn at different speeds and in different ways
- encourages active learning
- helps individuals accept responsibility for their own learning
- helps students to learn how to learn
- generates motivation and commitment
- dispels the idea that attendance in class is equivalent to effort and achievement.

The other benefits of open learning include:

- accessibility of time and place
- greater flexibility
- facilitates equality of opportunity
- helps maintain or create competitive advantage
- modular design for more focused use
- greater control over quality of training
- simulates safety procedures
- can be used to provide job aids.

Open learning is not a panacea for all training needs. Some are more appropriately met by 'live' training courses.

# 3 Making the most of a corporate learning centre

## Introduction

When considering how to make the most of a learning centre, the main issues are the identification of training needs, the drawing up of a relevant syllabus in response to those needs and the evaluation of training. Only the most job relevant and best quality courseware should be chosen for the centre. A good management information system will be needed for training records and general administration. It is important that the centre has the support of management and that access is made easy for staff.

## Identified training needs

As part of the annual business planning process, managers should examine individual training plans with their staff and identify training needs to meet their work programmes. Managers should consider if the corporate learning centre can meet their needs before sending their staff to external training establishments. Corporate learning centre courses may prove more cost effective. A detailed course catalogue should be provided for each manager so that they can decide to what extent their training needs can be met by corporate learning centre courses.

The section work programmes are tied to annual business plans which in turn are linked to the strategic objectives, so that training becomes part of the corporate planning process. Because staff are involved in the drawing up of individual training plans they are likely to be more committed to them and motivated to implement them. The participation of employees in the drawing up of individual training plans is an example of empowerment in action.

Open learning should be specifically targeted towards an identified training need. It should complement other training methods as it is unlikely to be an appropriate solution for all training needs. Managers should ensure that the corporate learning centre courses are relevant to their employees' current and future job needs or to their personal development and to the needs of the organization. Learners should be encouraged to reflect on how the knowledge and skills gained can be applied to their jobs.

# Syllabus

The style and content of the syllabus should reflect personal and organizational aims and the culture of the organization, and also tie in with existing training programmes. If the organization needs to improve information technology skills this should be apparent from the number of such courses on offer in the syllabus. Likewise, if the company has a big commitment to the personal development needs of staff. Employees who wish to study certificate, diploma and degree programmes to qualify should be offered a range of relevant academic course material. And the company that wishes to become more marketing oriented in its business approach will reflect this desire in the number of marketing and customer relations type courses available in the centre.

The syllabus should be available in two formats – a pocket-sized summary handbook called 'A guide to corporate learning centre courses for learners' and a detailed course catalogue for managers.

# Evaluation

Evaluation is the assessment of the total value of a training course in behavioural and financial terms. In other words, has the trainee acquired the required skill or knowledge and is the training good value for money? Evaluation should be at the following four levels:

● What are the opinions and attitudes of trainees to the learning experience?
● What new knowledge, skills and attitudes have they learnt?
● Have they applied this knowledge, skills and attitudes to their jobs?
● Has the efficiency, effectiveness and profitability of the company been improved as a direct result?

It is important that learners who use the corporate learning centre should complete end-of-course evaluation sheets. These can be used to monitor the quality, acceptability and relevance of course programmes. In addition, individual learners and their supervisors should be followed up after a time to gain a picture of the effectiveness of a particular package and the value of the centre as a learning resource. The following information should be established:

- Did the course meet the learner's expectations and was the learner able to apply the knowledge and skill acquired in the workplace?
- Was there a noticeable improvement in performance? Results may be evaluated at the departmental or corporate level by cost benefit analysis.
- What financial savings and other benefits are attributable directly to the course and are these greater than the cost of running the programme?

The information obtained from this continuous evaluation can be used to improve the services of the corporate learning centre and make the programmes more focused.

# Certification by outside bodies

Certification should be sought for certain programmes initially and extended to all courses if successful. It is an added attraction if courses are certified by an outside independent third-level college. For example, the corporate learning centre could be used to support staff doing the City and Guilds Certificate in Information Technology and Business Skills. The linking up of corporate learning centre courses with suitable distance learning programmes of third-level colleges at certificate, diploma and degree level is also a possibility. In fact, co-operative joint ventures between corporate learning centres and colleges should be encouraged.

# Courseware programmes

## Validation

Before purchase, packages should be validated by subject experts for:

- quality
- relevance
- user friendliness
- learning effectiveness
- accessibility to learners and
- value for money.

Subject experts might be staff employed in functional areas or specialist positions. Programmes should be subject to local management certification that they meet identified training needs.

The programmes chosen should be interesting, practical and job-related and should cover a wide range of suitable subject areas.

Screening programmes can be a time-consuming job which needs to be taken into account when planning a corporate learning centre. Selection and stocking of poor quality programmes can adversely affect the centre's image and reputation. One bad experience and a learner may not come back again. It is important that only the best quality courseware is stocked in the corporate learning centre.

## Choosing courseware

Consider the possibility of obtaining inspection copies or sample material from suppliers for evaluation before purchase. Most suppliers will send you a demo disk for preview on request, which will help you judge how good and interactive the courseware is. Select a few staff with expertise in the particular subject area to examine the courseware and give their views as to quality, standard and relevance. You could also visit suppliers and inspect the material. Many suppliers have viewing facilities on their premises. Another approach is to visit an organization which is already using a specific package and obtain feedback from them about the courseware's quality. Always weigh up the evaluation time against the cost and perceived importance of a programme.

## Bespoke courseware

An important consideration is whether to lease or buy programmes off the shelf or make them yourself. Because of the huge cost involved in creating in-house bespoke packages, this option is only feasible for large companies where a cost benefit analysis shows that such an approach is justified by the savings achieved as against the use of conventional training or the purchase of commercial off-the-shelf packages. In other words, it can be justified if the capital cost involved can be spread over a large number of users. However, in the last few years the range and quality of commercial off-the-shelf packages has improved enormously and the need for bespoke courseware has lessened. Some commercial packages can be customized at little extra cost to meet the specific needs of users.

## Quality of courseware

Studies have also shown, unsurprisingly, that learners like well-designed courseware but reject poor courseware. The quality of courseware will be measured according to: learner expectations; how old the ideas or presentation of the material appears to be; the relevance of the material to the learner's organization; the length or complexity of the material; its interactiveness; how graphical and attractive the material is and so on. Learners will like or dislike various materials according to their different learning styles.

## What makes a good package?

A good open learning package will enable a learner to work through the material alone and to learn quickly and effectively. It must anticipate and deal satisfactorily with the type of problems and questions the average open learner will experience without the benefit of a face-to-face tutor. In evaluating a open learning package, consider the following points:

- What level is it aimed at – beginners or advanced?
- What format best suits your purpose – text, audio, video, CBT, IV or CD-ROM?
- Is it supported by user friendly workbooks, if appropriate?
- Is it good value for money?
- Has it clear objectives, a modular structure and progress tests? Is it flexible? Can learners with different abilities and preferences take optional paths?
- Will it motivate the learner and sustain interest? Is it easy to understand and user friendly? Does it use graphics to good effect?
- Does it meet a particular training need? Is it in harmony with the company's overall training and development strategy?
- Does it do the job of an existing live programme and thus free trainers for more demanding work?

## Winning acceptability for open learning

How will employees react to the notion of a corporate learning centre, with its emphasis on self-learning, self-reliance and use of information technology? Will it become a hive of activity or a white elephant – an under-utilized resource? Some companies have adopted corporate learning centres not on cost grounds, nor to meet training and development needs, and with little or no thought of how the centre should be supported or maintained. Where this is the case and senior management commitment dries up, the centre will gradually die.

The mission and purpose of the learning centre must be studied and linked with the overall training and development strategy and corporate objectives of the company. The practical implications should be examined and how it will be integrated and used as part of an overall training plan. A senior manager with a particular vision and interest in learning should be given the task of ensuring that the centre succeeds in the company's mission of providing lifelong learning opportunities that will benefit both the company and its employees. Similarly, in a multisite situation, a local manager should be responsible for the success of the centre.

Many organizations have found that clerical, administrative and professional staff, who are usually computer literate, take to computer-based training with great ease. After some initial guidance and tutor-based support they become self-sufficient open learners after a short time and need only the minimum of tutor intervention. Manual workers may require more help because of their lack of a conceptual framework and familiarity with information technology and personal computers. Some may fear computers. Help should be provided by the corporate learning centre coordinator who can gradually bring them to an appreciation of computers with encouragement and sensitivity.

There are now very good video-based computer appreciation courses which can be used to ease the process of induction and build up the learners' basic knowledge, confidence and frame of reference in computers. From these video courses, learners could graduate to a CBT course on keyboarding skills. Interactive video courses on computer appreciation with touch screen technology could be given to the computer phobic learners. Some of these programmes are specially designed for learners to overcome an initial fear of computers.

## Tapping personal development needs

To attract customers to the corporate learning centre, programmes of a social, recreational and personal development nature should also be stocked. The coordinator can then draw their attention to the wide range of other courses available. Personal development subjects are often popular, for example, psychology courses dealing with interpersonal relations, self-esteem, assertiveness and confidence. Most of these courses are on audio and videotapes. This format is ideal for the person seeking to study in their own time. Some use personal stereos for listening to the audiotapes, while others listen on their car stereos as they commute to and from work.

The needs of part-time students should also be catered for. This is a growing area with many employees studying on a part-time basis for certificate, diploma, degree and post-degree level with universities and professional institutes. There are a growing number of open learning programmes available for their specific needs and these should be stocked in the corporate learning centre. Many companies operate an educational support scheme to assist these students to finance their studies.

## Encouraging employees

The usage of the corporate learning centre should be monitored, which could include checking the number of loans to learners including text, audio and video programmes for self-study at home. The centre should aim to attract as wide a section of employees as possible, including operatives, clerical, accounting, administrative, supervisory, management, engineering and technical categories. Occasional fall off in usage of the centre might be counteracted by an aggressive advertising and marketing drive as appropriate.

## Encouraging managers

Sometimes managers may be resistant to using the corporate learning centre. They may lack keyboarding skills and be unfamiliar with the basic equipment and peripherals. They don't want to look foolish in front of their computer-literate younger colleagues. Managers should be encouraged to study basic keyboarding and computer courses. New employees straight from college are likely to be computer literate and will have no hesitation in using the resources of the centre which may be a source of embarrassment to managers.

Managers are often under a lot of work pressure. They may feel that time spent away from their desks in a corporate learning centre would not be looked on favourably by their peers and superiors – 'If he has time for open learning, maybe he's underemployed'. This attitude is regrettable. Managers more than anyone else should be seen to be updating their skills and keeping abreast of new thinking in business and management. Senior managers should encourage middle managers and supervisors to include corporate learning centre courses as part of their training and development as well as undertaking such courses themselves.

Managers should be setting an example to their staff that lifelong learning is important for individuals and for the company and is recognized as such. They should be the driving force in creating and sustaining a learning culture in the organization. It is a contradiction that senior managers authorize a huge financial investment in corporate learning centres and then subsequently fail to support them in any visible fashion, either by allowing their staff time off to attend the centre or by using it themselves.

## Accessibility

The corporate learning centre should be accessible to all employees and open at least during normal working hours. Ideally, it should open daily from 9am to 9pm although this may not be possible because of the cost of staffing. Outside of these times, or normal working hours, the centre could be accessed by a special electronic magnetic card. This swipe card could be numerically controlled and issued to staff who request use of the centre after normal working hours.

'Smart' cards are available that will update the corporate learning centre's management information system. This will give the coordinator information on who used the centre, which course they undertook, the duration of the course and so on. This facility will be particularly useful for shiftworkers who need to plan their open learning around their working hours. With proper organization and planning the centre may provide a 24-hour round-the-clock service.

## Sharing facilities

The capacity of the corporate learning centre can also be shared with other locations. In large regional-based organizations, open learning allows employees to obtain training in isolated locations where, because of inadequate demand, traditional training courses would be uneconomic. Computer networks means that there is now no limit to the range of training courses that can be made available irrespective of the location. All you need is a PC and the right telecommunications infrastructure in place. These days most employees have access to a computer in their workplace. Each PC is a potential mini corporate learning centre in its own right and can be linked to PCs in the main centre.

## Manager's role

Line managers should demonstrate their commitment to open learning and interest their staff by asking them for their views on the corporate learning centre courses and where they hope to apply the knowledge. They should also be encouraged to discuss the courses with their colleagues. Word of mouth recommendation may introduce new customers to the centre. Corporate learning centre courses may be used as an introductory or refresher process for both knowledge and skills areas.

Managers should integrate open learning courses into the work routine by allowing staff to attend courses. Staff should be briefed before they go on courses and debriefed when they return. This displays an ongoing interest on the managers' part in the development of their staff. Managers should ensure that open learning is linked to better on-the-job performance, career progression and development. It should become standard practice at internal promotion interviews to ask candidates about open learning programmes undertaken and their application to on-the-job situations.

Pedagogy is a learning philosophy which assumes that the learner has a dependent personality. On the other hand, in andragogy the learner is assumed to be seeking increasing self-direction. The andragogic approach is more suitable in a work context. However, it should not be assumed that learners will voluntarily want to engage in corporate learning centre courses. They must have a reason for undertaking such programmes and the organizational climate must be supportive. Managers are an important catalyst in this process.

## Use it or lose it

Unless learners revise or apply knowledge or skill shortly after acquisition they will lose it. To retain the skill it must also be applied frequently. The corporate learning centre, close to the workplace, is a great way to refresh existing knowledge and keep abreast of new developments. It may be used to acquire knowledge and skill on a particular topic before attending a traditional 'live' course. Because the learners have built up a conceptual framework of the material they will find it easier to learn.

## Open learning and the bottom line

The provision of a corporate learning centre is a practical demonstration of the organization's commitment to staff training and development and visible evidence of learner empowerment. In practice the concept of learner empowerment through open learning will be constrained by commercial and organizational factors, including the need to meet specified training objectives in line with corporate goals and to translate them into relevant improvements in work practices and visible cost savings.

Hard-nosed managers with their eye on the bottom line often require tangible benefits for any investment in training. In times of recession budgetary constraints will be a real problem as cutbacks bite into the training budget. Open learning must be shown to make a positive contribution by the quality of its courses and the transferability of the acquired skills to practical work situations. Line managers should be involved in the selection of suitable courseware to meet the identified training needs in their areas of responsibility.

## Management information systems

Good software packages are available commercially for managing the administrative requirements of a corporate learning centre. These packages cover the recording of booking in learners, such as time, type and description of course and booth allocated, as well as keeping tabs on learners' progress and recording loans and returns of books, audio and video tapes.

They also provide comprehensive management information for individual training records and usage level of the courses. This information may be used to compare standards, popularity and job relevancy of programmes and the numbers and types of employees who are using the corporate learning centres. If the company has many centres in its organization then comparative statistics may be compiled to see which are the most successful and why.

Carefully collated information will show which medium is the most popular – text, audio, video, CBT, CD-ROM or IV. More importantly, it will highlight who is not using the centre and will help to focus marketing drives on those segments of employees. Programmes not being used should be weeded out and discarded. Job-relevant courses or popular subject areas should be purchased. It is important that corporate learning centres do not deteriorate into museums. The courses should be current, job relevant and frequently used.

## Organizations with corporate learning centres

Corporate learning centres are now a well established means for training in progressive organizations in the UK and Ireland. Littlefield (1994) reports that the UK is now said to be the leader in computer-based training. Rover has spent £2 million setting up its own open learning mini-enterprise, Rover Learning Business. Elsewhere in the UK, Lucas, British Steel, British Telecom and Norwich Union have all established corporate learning centres. The majority of users tend to be large private or public sector organizations. In Ireland, centres have been set up in such companies as Aer Lingus, Electricity Supply Board, FAS (The Irish Training Authority), Bank of Ireland, AIB Bank and Ulster Bank.

In the US, Marx (1995) reports that 80 per cent of the Fortune 500 companies are using interactive multimedia training. According to *Training* magazine, 20 per cent of the 2,000 plus companies completing its 1994 survey report using interactive video. Kay (1995) reports that Target Stores, a division of Carter Hawley Hale Stores of Los Angeles, uses computer-based training to make its training consistent over 600 stores.

*Training and Development* magazine (December 1994), reports that at Pacific Bell, an interactive multimedia programme called Employee Knowledge Link trains employees about the company's products and operating procedures. Using digital networks, the system can deliver training materials consisting of text, graphics, photographic images, audio and video to 300 workstations scattered across California.

Fox (1994) reports that Dominick's Finer Foods, a Chicago-based group of supermarkets, uses CBT to train cashiers. Each of the 102 Dominick's stores has its own CBT system connected to the mainframe at head office. They found that their employees learn better from CBT than classroom instruction. They are now trying to market the system to other supermarket groups.

# Summary

To make the most of your corporate learning centre you must:

- identify training needs
- draw up a relevant syllabus to meet those needs
- evaluate open learning courses
- ensure that only the most job relevant and best quality courseware is selected and stocked
- obtain certification of some of your courses by linking up with outside colleges
- cater for the personal development needs of staff
- ensure employees' easy access to the centre during and after normal working hours
- make the most of your management information system
- encourage your managers to actively support the learning centre.

# 4 Establishing costs and measuring benefits

## Introduction

The costs of a corporate learning centre may be considered under two headings – capital expenditure and revenue expenditure. Capital expenditure is the cost of setting up and equipping the centre, while revenue expenditure is the cost of running the centre. You will need two budgets to control costs:

- a capital expenditure budget for equipment and premises, and
- a revenue or operating cost budget for software, overheads and running expenses.

The following sections will consider these costs in detail. It is useful to know the comparative costs of the various media used in open learning and to be aware of some of the success stories of the application of open learning in organizations.

## Capital expenditure

Capital expenditure is the cost of setting up and equipping the centre. It includes premises, furniture and fittings, booths for learners, computer hardware and other equipment costs such as printers, television sets, CD-ROM players, audio-cassette players and video players. There will also be the costs of fitting out the premises, including special electrical wiring, painting, carpets, plants and pictures. To become operational, capital expenditure may range from £20,000 to £100,000 depending on the number of booths, equipment and size of the accommodation.

# Revenue expenditure

Revenue expenditure will include the coordinator's salary, light and heat, depreciation of equipment, maintenance and repair of premises and equipment, rent and rates, telephone charges, postage, stationery, cleaning and software costs. Annual revenue expenditure or running costs, assuming a full time coordinator, may be around £60,000 in an average centre. The size of this budget will be strongly influenced by the number, variety and quality of courseware that you intend to stock in the corporate learning centre.

# Budget

A capital expenditure budget for equipment and a revenue expenditure budget for software and the operating costs of running the centre must be drawn up each year by the coordinator, who will agree it with the training and development manager. The management information system should provide monthly reports on budgets and actual amounts spent. These should be examined each month to ensure that costs are on target and that any overexpenditure is investigated and accounted for.

# Marketing costs

Marketing costs will be an important element in the corporate learning centre's budget. There will be a one-off marketing cost when launching the centre. Ongoing costs will include advertising in the form of the users' course guide, managers' course guide, brochures, posters, e-mail, and the cost of the quarterly newsletter. A competent coordinator may be able to do the marketing and thus keep costs down but some outside printing costs, such as the course guides, may be inevitable.

# Videotapes

Training videotapes vary in cost from £100 to as much as £1,500. High price is not always synonymous with good quality. They include workbooks and or trainer's and participants' guides. Some are designed as training packages which can be run as 'live' workshops or worked through individually by learners.

## Audiotapes

A single audiotape may cost £10 or less. Training packages consisting of six or more audiotapes complete with workbooks may cost considerably more, but still offer good value for money. A budget of a few thousand pounds will stock the corporate learning centre with a good selection of audio programmes. But beware! Although there are many excellent audiotapes on the market, there are also poor quality programmes being sold, so make sure you evaluate them before purchase.

## Text-based courses

Books may cost as little as £5. Text-based courses consisting of trainer's and participants' guides cost considerably more, perhaps up to £150 per course. Don't be blinded by the hype about multimedia or technology-based training. Text-based resources remain a highly cost-effective development tool. Many learners still prefer working with books and their needs should be catered for. Again, a budget of a few thousand pounds could stock the learning centre with a good quality and variety of course material.

## CBT

Computer-based training costs should be compared to the equivalent cost of sending someone on a training course. A large number of employees can do the same course with significant savings. Good CBT programmes may cost as much as £3,000. Prices generally depend on how interactive and graphical the courseware and good lower cost programmes are available. If you have a number of corporate learning centres you may be able to obtain a licence from the supplier which will work out much cheaper. Where there is a large number of individuals using a CBT programme the cost per trainee will be modest. A word of warning is needed in relation to CBT, as with video – high price does not guarantee good quality. Check out the CBT courseware before purchase.

CBT may be perceived as an expensive option but there are plenty of examples which suggest that it is cost effective. Fuller and Saunders (1990) report that British Telecom estimated costs of £40 million to train its 20,000 operators to use computerized telephone exchanges. However, instead of spending £40 million, BT bought a CBT system for £4 million and thus made a saving of £36 million. Lougher (1988) says that British Steel is currently investing more than £20 million a year in various training activities. Open learning accounts for about £2 million of this. It recognizes that its continuing success will largely depend on maintaining this investment policy.

Forlenza (1995) reports that the average initial cost of implementing a

CBT programme, including hardware, is $8 per employee per hour of training – compared to an average of $50 for conventional classroom training. Cost efficiency improves as more employees use the system – CBT costs are one-time; classroom costs are incurred each time a training course is run.

## Multimedia

The cost of multimedia packages including CD-ROM and interactive video tends to be higher than CBT. Most such packages start at about £1,000 and can go up to £10,000 or more. You have to judge this cost in relation to the number of trainees that will use the programme and the savings involved against traditional training. The main cost of multimedia is in design and production. In traditional training the costs are in travel, accommodation, disruption of work, overtime, trainer/learner time, stationery and capital depreciation. For bespoke multimedia packages the breakeven point is probably between 100 and 200 learners. With off-the-shelf courseware it can be as little as 10 learners. Above these figures significant savings are achieved. Plan for a budget of £20,000 or more for multimedia.

The computer hardware for IV is much more expensive than for CBT and CD-ROM and the programmes themselves are often high cost. To be cost effective, a bespoke IV programme needs to be relevant to 250 learners or more, so small companies are unlikely to find it a viable proposition. Planned improvements in CD-ROM may reduce further the advantages of IV and eventually supersede it.

## Authoring systems

Authoring systems are available for trainers to use, but they require considerable time to become proficient in. For example, Kattackal (1994) reports that a trainer typically takes 100 to 150 hours to produce each delivered hour of CBT and six to nine months to develop a moderately complex multimedia course. Costs of authoring software range from a few hundred to a few thousand dollars. If the trainer uses video extensively, costs could reach as much as $150,000 to $250,000, or about $10,000 to $20,000 per finished hour of training. Therefore, it is only the bigger companies which could afford to do their own courseware design as the cost for even modest programmes is likely to run into thousands of pounds. There is always the possibility of subcontracting the work to an outside software house. In any event, the expense of designing your own courseware can only be justified on a cost benefit basis where large numbers of employees will use it and thus the cost per trainee will become economical.

Authoring programmes using existing off-the-shelf video or other materials is likely to contravene the original producer's copyright and may prove a legal minefield.

# Profitability

Like any other business undertaking learning centres should be run on a commercial basis as profit centres. To make them cost transparent and commercially viable there should be a charge for internal departments and the centre should also be marketed externally. There are many different ways in which a charge could be made. Some companies may see the corporate learning centre as a cost centre and thus be satisfied with a recovery of costs. The centre might therefore be charged to the user departments on bases such as number of employees or take up of courses.

Other companies might like to treat the corporate learning centre on a more commercial basis and charge market rates for its services. Initially they could be opened to staff family members on a fee-paying basis and eventually opened up commercially to employees of other organizations. Off-the-shelf materials are sold for use within the purchasing organization only. Organizations wishing to open their centre to other organizations or individuals should check the situation with the producers of the material they have purchased to avoid experiencing copyright litigation.

# Cost savings

One of the main motivations behind the introduction of corporate learning centres is cost savings. Studies suggest that open learning is more cost effective than traditional training. It saves trainer time and learner time off the job. As a learning medium it is also more effective in some instances than other forms of training. Retention rates are higher and learning is integrated into the job faster and better when it occurs near the workplace rather than 'away on a course'. However, line managers must be convinced by concrete evidence that corporate learning centres are cost effective and do in fact meet real training needs.

The financial benefits of training are difficult to quantify. Nevertheless, it is important to quantify the savings and benefits of a corporate learning centre. In fact, the costs are relatively easy to establish. The management information system will contain information on the number of learners, courses taken, duration of courses, popularity of courses, media used and so on. From the corporate learning centre budgets and this information it will be possible to work out the cost per trainee hour. Comparisons can then be made with 'live' training conducted within the company or outside and can be used to prove the cost effectiveness of learning centre courses, i.e. the reduced cost of training. The financial savings in:

- travelling
- overnight accommodation
- reduced overtime
- less absence from the workplace
- and other costs

can easily be quantified. Other benefits such as:

- improvements in productivity
- increased job satisfaction and morale
- improved quality
- better customer service
- increased confidence of employees and
- improved career prospects

may be more difficult to quantify but nevertheless should be considered.

## Measuring the benefits

In general the training provided by the corporate learning centre should be seen as a long-term investment and vote of confidence in people rather than as a cost. Although not reflected directly on the balance sheet of a company it is in fact an investment in intellectual capital and will enhance the company's ability to make profits. It is more valuable than brands which are often capitalized on the balance sheet. This enhancement in intellectual capital has a real value and may be quantified in management accounts just as some companies do for brands in the financial accounts. The investment in intellectual capital will reap many benefits in the future including a knowledge-based added value which will prove to be the key competitive advantage in an information-driven society. It is the creativity, skill and knowledge of the workforce which will make the profits for the company and determine its success or failure.

Surveys of open learners and their managers will establish satisfaction levels with the corporate learning centre. In particular the coordinator should receive feedback on actual applications and benefits of open learning courses to on-the-job situations. Managers might be asked to quantify any financial savings achieved. On the basis of this feedback improvements should be made to the range of courses and services offered by the centre. The centre's philosophy should be to make continuous improvement in the range of courses and services on offer. It is also necessary to keep in touch with what is happening in the outside world. This can be through contact with other companies using corporate learning centres, colleges involved in computer-based training, suppliers, user associations and courseware exhibitions. The Internet may assist in this process.

From the management information system statistics may be compiled of the numbers using the centre, the types of courses used, popularity, their frequency and duration. A top ten list of the most popular courses can be identified and, more importantly, the least popular can be marked out for possible removal. This information can be classified by department, division, grade of employee, age, gender and so on. It will be invaluable in discovering the areas of the company which are benefiting from corporate learning centre courses.

# Companies claiming benefits and savings

Open learning may be a cost effective way of bringing training to those who need it most. Chute (1990) highlights an AT & T study which showed that the actual cost of technology-based training is lower than traditional training.

Organizations such as British Steel have found investment in corporate learning centres to be cost effective. Lougher (1988) says British Steel reckons that to set up a small learning centre costs about £20,000 while a larger unit would cost about £75,000. They make their own IV and CBT programmes and find them very cost effective. The cost of developing computer courseware is high and can only be justified if it can be spread over a large number of trainees.

Fuller and Saunders (1990) say that companies such as Sainsbury's, B&Q, Austin Rover, Lucas and Jaguar in the UK have found corporate learning centres to be a good investment. Managers argue that the initial costs of installing new equipment and buying or producing course materials are offset by less need for trainers, and savings. This is because staff learn either in their own time or at work instead of off-site in the company's training college or attending external training establishments.

Ferrar (1991) highlights the case of Bradford & Bingley Building Society in the UK that was awarded its second National Training Award in November 1990. The winning open learning programme reached more than 750 staff and used text-based packages, audio cassettes, interactive video and workshops. The programme's aim was to train all branch staff in the skills of marketing the society's lending services, and it was so successful that lending at the society rose to record levels.

Littlefield (1994) reports that Rank Xerox claims to have saved millions of dollars as a result of heavy investment in interactive video and CD-ROM. The company is using multimedia to train service engineers in maintenance skills. They can simulate the assembly of pieces of machinery on screen. This compares to working on expensive printers costing up to £30,000 each. Rank Zerox has also set up a corporate learning centre in Poland to train 50 east European recruits to western standards in customer care, management, business and computer skills.

Marx (1995) reports that interactive media's biggest appeal may be its potential to cut training costs. While it can cost anywhere from $50,000 to several millions of dollars to develop an interactive multimedia programme, depending on its size and scope, the savings are significant as soon as the courseware is developed. This is because companies save the costs they would ordinarily incur on travelling, hotels and trainers. By offering its business practice course as an interactive multimedia programme, Arthur Anderson estimates that it has saved $10.5 million a year over its traditional classroom programme costs.

## Cutbacks in training budgets

In every annual report organizations refer to the key role people play in the success of their business. However, the same organizations are often reluctant and sceptical about investing in those people through training and development programmes. In fact in times of recession one of the first budgets to be reduced or indeed eliminated is the training and development budget. This is because it is so easy to cut and seemingly painless. Its cost reduction consequences are felt immediately, but the strategic implications of a reduction in training may not be felt for some years.

Many commentators see the German vocational training system as an important component of their economic success. Similar claims have been made for the Japanese approach to training. On the other hand the British and Irish attitude to training leaves a lot to be desired as reflected in their much smaller investment in training. Training must be taken seriously if countries are to make a successful transition to the knowledge-based society and compete successfully with the Germans and Japanese.

## Summary

The costs of establishing and running a corporate learning centre can be classified under the two headings of capital expenditure and revenue expenditure. Capital expenditure is the cost of setting up the centre and acquiring the premises and equipment. Revenue expenditure is the operating cost and will include marketing costs. The different costs associated with the various media used in open learning were highlighted. In addition, the costs and benefits of running a corporate learning centre were identified and examples given of some companies who claim significant savings and benefits as a result of their use.

# 5     How to resolve resistance to change

## Introduction

In the modern world organizations are faced with rapid change – political, legal, economic, social, technological and competitive. Organizations can ignore change and risk extinction or actively decide to manage change. A proactive approach to training and development is needed to maintain a competitive advantage. New technology has provided new delivery systems for education and training. It would be very short-sighted to ignore these developments. The corporate learning centre approach is an essential ingredient of any progressive training and development strategy, a useful addition to the range of training resources and a positive response to managing change.

There are many reasons why employees might resist the idea of learning through corporate learning centres. These include natural resistance to change, fear of the unknown, work pressures, an unsupportive organizational climate, lack of learning skills, poor motivation, unenthusiastic management, special needs and domestic or other commitments. This chapter will explore these resistances in some detail and suggest ways in which they might be overcome.

## Force field analysis

A useful model for understanding change is force field analysis. This technique can be used for anticipating, analysing and understanding the various forces acting for and against change. If you anticipate and plan for change then you can be prepared for the likely arguments against it. In this model change is seen as the outcome of some forces which tend to bring about change and other forces which tend to resist change. Change is helped through the reduction or elimination of the resisting forces and through a strengthening of the driving forces.

## The driving forces of change

The driving forces might include:

- competition means that the company must make its training more cost effective
- the need for employee training in information technology skills
- the need to decentralize training and make it available to all employees
- employee desire for empowerment
- support of boardroom management.

## The restraining forces of change

The restraining forces might include:

- company culture is bureaucratic and resists any change
- managers are sceptical about open learning
- trainers see open learning as a threat to their jobs
- initial capital investment is high and the return seen as uncertain
- no existing tradition or experience in the company of computer-based training

Figure 5.1 shows the result of a force field analysis on the situation. A number of restraining forces have been identified and the relative importance of each shown in relation to the arrowed line (longer lines imply more importance). In this example the effective implementation of a corporate learning centre will be restrained by the culture of the company and the scepticism of managers about open learning, the resistance of trainers who see open learning as a threat to their jobs, the high capital investment required and the uncertain return. Similarly, a number of driving forces have also been identified, including the need to maintain competitiveness, pressure from boardroom management, the desire to decentralize training.

The decision maker can now use the analysis to evaluate how the restraining factors might be removed or reduced and how to reinforce the driving forces.

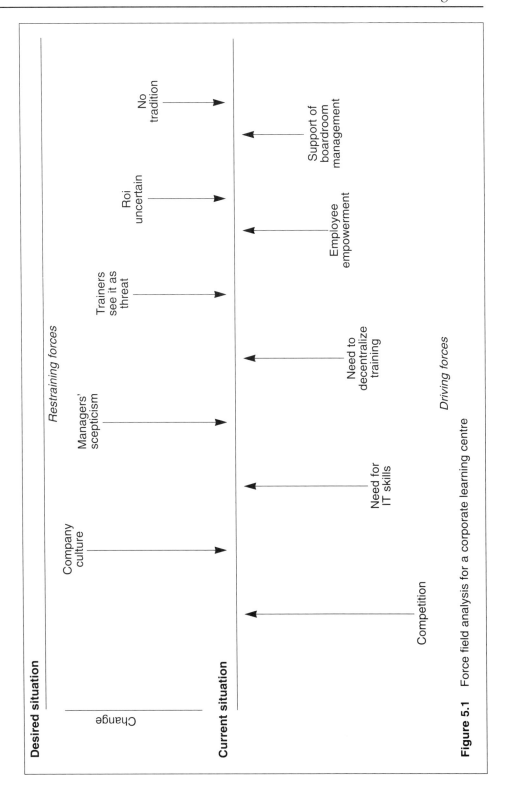

**Figure 5.1**   Force field analysis for a corporate learning centre

## Wrong organizational climate

| *Indicator* | *Reason* |
|---|---|
| Lack of top management support. | Senior managers see training as a cost rather than an investment. They prefer to buy in staff with the necessary expertise. |
| Initial top management support which then wanes | Senior managers initially support open learning and the creation of a centre, not because they believe in the centre but because they perceive it as cheaper than traditional training. |
| Managers pay lip-service to the centre but then fail to support it themselves, fail to encourage staff to use the centre and even make it difficult for staff to put aside time for learning. | The managers have not been convinced of the real benefit to their team of open learning. This may be because of a perceived lack of support amongst senior managers. |
| Managers and supervisors actively discourage staff from using the centre. | Lack of direction from senior managers. Fear that well-trained staff may either be a threat to them or that these staff will move to other companies or be poached. |
| Managers and supervisors are short-term oriented. Their immediate priorities relate to getting the work done in their own sections. | They lack the vision that the company will have skills needs and management succession needs in the future and that training and development is vitally important for the strategic success of the company. |
| Managers feel that training raises the expectations of staff which cannot be met. | The current delayering policy of many organizations means that there will be less opportunities for promotion in the future. So overqualified staff could feel frustrated and disillusioned. |

Resolving these problems is not easy, but it is essential to win support from senior and middle management, and to develop the right climate for learning within the organization before you start, if the centre is to have any hope of succeeding. The following techniques will help to resolve the problems.

# Top management briefing

First, it is important to sell the concept fully to senior managers. They need to understand:

- what the centre can and cannot offer to employees and the organization
- the strengths and weaknesses of computer-based training
- what the set up and running costs will be
- how the centre will fit into the context of training within the organization
- what impact it will have on the hours worked by employees using the centre, and
- what the future strategy of the centre is likely to be.

At this stage you should encourage all and any questions and establish support. If you can obtain support from the senior managers to concrete action, such as their commitment to brief managers and staff to visit the centre themselves, then so much the better.

Their initial commitment is only the first step. You will need to brief them regularly on your progress. The statistics you gather on usage of the centre, along with any feedback and research from users and their managers, will all provide you with evidence of the growing impact and success of the centre.

# Middle managers

Briefing the middle managers might be done in an informal way, perhaps by chatting with them individually in the canteen or buttonholing individuals for five minutes when they arrive at work. It is just as important as the top management briefing.

Once again, you need to ensure that the managers understand what the centre can offer them and their staff. They will have to understand and give their commitment to supporting their staff, by allowing them time to learn, encouraging them to use the centre and taking an active interest in their development. This would include follow-up action to ensure that staff regularly attend relevant corporate learning centre courses to meet identified training needs and corporate strategic requirements. You may choose to remind managers that they have line responsibility for the training and development of their staff. Potential learners look to their managers as role models, so encourage the managers themselves to use and enthuse about the centre.

## Participation councils

Many large companies use participation councils as a channel of communication with employees. Council members are often the informal leaders of work groups and thus a great channel through which to promulgate the benefits of open learning generally in the company. Emphasise that open learning can help employees' job skills, personal development and career prospects. The important benefit of accessibility for all employees regardless of age, status or previous education should also be stressed.

## Trainer's resistance to change

Resistance to change will not only come from potential customers but is also likely to come from training staff themselves. They may see the introduction of corporate learning centres into the company as a threat to their jobs. It is true that some forms of training may be undertaken more cost effectively through open learning. However, this should be seen as complementary to, rather than a substitute for, live training. It will free trainers to concentrate on the more difficult, demanding, practical and more company specific aspects, such as the identification of training needs and the evaluation of training. It will also give them an opportunity to develop their mentoring and coaching roles. They can at last take on the role of facilitator rather than instructor.

Much of the knowledge and theory aspects of training programmes may be delegated to the corporate learning centre. As part of group training programmes, participants can be told to work through relevant open learning courseware before they come on the 'live' training course. The time span of such courses can thus be reduced and trainers will have more time to concentrate on the more challenging and interactive aspects of training such as projects, case studies, role play, interpersonal relations skills and teamwork. This job enrichment will provide more satisfaction for the trainer and ultimately reduce the direct cost of live training which becomes more focused and relevant. In addition, preparation time and the cost of producing handouts and transparencies is saved.

The message must be understood by trainers – there is no threat to their jobs. The only difference will be that their jobs will become more interesting as the routine aspects of training will be taken over by the corporate learning centre. Any reduction in the number of trainers should be through natural wastage and non-replacement. This will free the trainers to develop new skills and to concentrate on the more demanding and interesting aspects of training and develop their facilitating role.

## Learner's resistance to change

There is a natural resistance to change in most people. They prefer to keep on doing what they're used to doing. In psychology this is known as the comfort zone. Mature people, in particular, seem to prefer routine and sometimes fear the inevitable arrival of the new information technology. This is unlike the younger generation which has grown up with PCs and treat them as an ordinary everyday gadget like television or any other modern appliance.

Good communications, education, training and marketing should be part of the battle to change attitudes and overcome this resistance to the use of information technology and open learning in particular. Open learning should be part of the approach to equip employees to cope with change.

### Reluctant employees

Some staff lack the intrinsic motivation to undertake any formal new learning experience. They are content with their lot, lack ambition and thus don't see the necessity for undertaking any open learning courses. They know how to do their existing jobs, so why bother with anything else? They don't seem to realize that there are now no guarantees of jobs for life and that new skills must be developed on an ongoing basis if one is to survive in the modern workplace. In fact, the more skills you possess the more marketable you will become, not only to your own employer but to potential outside employers as well. These staff require special consideration and incentives to use the corporate learning centres. They are probably the ones who need training the most but are the least likely to receive it. One way around this problem might be to give such staff monetary incentives to do corporate learning centre courses. Certainly, managers and supervisors should particularly encourage these employees.

### Fear

Another barrier is a psychological fear of any formalized new learning, including open learning and traditional training. Many people fear any form of institutional learning. This could be a throwback to schooldays with associations of failure, inferiority, punishment, teacher/authority figures, competition and classrooms. The prospect of 'making a fool of themselves' or appearing 'stupid' in front of peers in a traditional training situation can deter them from attending a course. One of the great advantages of open learning is that you can make your mistakes in private. No one need know about them and nobody is breathing down your neck.

Of course, learning from your mistakes is the best way to effective learning.

A middle-aged person who wants to learn new skills may feel inadequate, uncomfortable and threatened on a 'live' course with much younger people. However, with the right support, encouragement and a favourable environment they often become the best, most committed and motivated of open learners. Learning is often wasted on the young who do not savour the opportunity to enhance their education and training.

Corporate learning centres provide a non-threatening, supportive environment for learners with none of the competition and stress associated with traditional training. Nevertheless, some learners fear the unstructured nature of open learning. It is important that the coordinator informs the learner of the difference between traditional training and open learning and stresses the benefits of the latter. The coordinator should be supportive and facilitative rather than intrusive. The learner will appreciate the opportunity to experiment with new ideas and approaches without peer pressure or trainer interference.

## Domestic commitments

For many adults, work is not their only responsibility. Their families also need consideration and demand attention. For personal success, harmony and happiness individuals need to create balance in their lives. There is a time to work and a time to play. Time for yourself and your family is important. Working parents may find difficulty in arranging childcare or crèche facilities to attend courses that require travel and overnight stays.

Corporate learning centre courses can be taken at a time which suits parents' working arrangements, domestic situations and lifestyle. Managers and supervisors should have regard to employee lifestyles and try to accommodate their needs with individual training plans which make use of the accessibility and flexibility of corporate learning centre courses. They should be generous in their approach to allowing such employees time off during the working day to attend such courses. It may be a good idea to provide crèche facilities adjacent to the corporate learning centre for employees with children. This certainly would be visible support on the company's part.

## Work pressures

Many employees have difficulty finding time to do corporate learning centre courses during the working day and are too tired to do so during their free time. Tight staffing arrangements and work deadlines mean this may sometimes be a problem in functional departments but is particularly acute in operational areas.

Some flexibility in staffing arrangements is needed to facilitate staff in operational areas to take up open learning. In practice large companies and public sector organizations tend to be more flexible in this area than smaller firms. An allowance of two hours per week per employee for relevant open learning courses would not seem unreasonable. For important courses a more generous block of time may be allocated, depending on the nature of the course and how relevant and urgent it is to the requirements of the job.

## Learners with special needs

Although there have been vast improvements in access to buildings in recent years, it can still be very difficult for people with physical disabilities to attend traditional courses in training and educational establishments. Making arrangements for special transport can add to the problems.

These problems are mostly overcome with corporate learning centres. At the design and planning stage of the centre the necessary modifications should be considered to cater for the physically disabled. Subsequent alterations may prove to be very expensive. An organization which cares for the training needs of physically disabled employees is seen as caring and progressive and will not hesitate to invest in their needs.

Conventional computer-based training programmes are not suitable for the deaf or blind or those with poor literacy and numeracy skills. Specially designed computer-based technology is available to help the visually impaired and the deaf to learn. In addition, there are very good programmes designed to help people with poor literacy and numeracy skills.

## Lack of study skills

Staff who have been away from formal learning situations for a long time may feel they lack the study skills, time management skills, willpower, concentration and mental discipline necessary to do an open learning programme. Many may not have any conventional educational qualifications or have undertaken any formal systematic study in the past. A CBT programme on study skills called *Learning to Learn* is available which staff can work through before they undertake a corporate learning centre course. There are also many very good books on study and learning skills available, including the author's *Learning to Learn* published by CIMA of London. Corporate learning centres should stock them and encourage newcomers to use them.

## Isolation

Learners may feel a sense of isolation when undertaking corporate learning centre courses and miss the social interaction, teamwork, comradeship, contact and stimulation of 'live' training. In fact, our whole education system has taught us to be passive rather than self-directed active learners. It takes some time to get used to the idea that we are responsible for our own learning and it requires a radical change of attitude on our part. People must learn to learn themselves and not wait around for other people to show them.

The 'drop in and help yourself to learning' philosophy of the corporate learning centre should overcome the attitude of dependence on others for learning. Tutorial support from the centre's coordinator may also help to alleviate the problem. Shlechter (1990) found that small group CBT was more cost effective than individual CBT by a factor of five and that learning effectiveness was increased. This would suggest that the coordinator might encourage learners to work in pairs which would reduce isolation while improving performance. Learners might also be encouraged to set up self-help groups to overcome the isolation problem. Support may also come from specialist experts in the organization, line managers and mentors.

## Boredom

It is a well established fact that the span of attention is between 20 and 40 minutes. Short breaks every half hour or so should be part of any learner's course in the corporate learning centre. Breaks maximize retention and learning and provide time for reflection and consolidation of learning. Programmes selected for the centre should be modular in structure, colourful, graphical and interactive with plenty of feedback in order to maintain concentration and interest and reduce boredom.

The CD-ROM courses now available use all the advantages of multimedia with colour, sound, graphics and moving pictures. A picture speaks more than a thousand words. Colour enhances memory, while variety helps to maintain attention and concentration. Many of these courses use the latest ideas from educational technology, are very interactive and thus optimize the learning process and prevent boredom.

## Confidence

In practice some people lack the confidence and self-esteem required to undertake any form of open learning course. They will have to be weaned gradually to the open learning idea and given a lot of support and guidance from the beginning.

Initially, to break them in, encourage them to take audio- and video-based programmes. Eventually they may develop the confidence to progress further and do some IV, CBT and CD-ROM-based courses. However, such people must be handled with a lot of patience, sensitivity and care. They should be made aware that learning a new subject is not easy but requires application, practice and persistence over time if they are to become successful and that most people going back to learning after many years' absence have feelings of inadequacy.

## Enabling learners to be effective

Research shows that learners require the following basic skills if they want to learn effectively:

- They should be motivated, in other words have a clear reason and purpose for learning. The coordinator and mentors can assist in this process.
- They need clear objectives. Learners learn more effectively if they have an overview of the topic and clear objectives to aim for.
- They need to operate to a plan. Time schedules with interim goals and objectives should be a feature of the plan, with rewards for the achievement of objectives.
- They need feedback on progress during the learning process. This might include tests, questionnaires and checklists which are an inbuilt feature of good computer-based training programmes.
- The learning must be relevant to their current or future needs.
- They should be able to learn at their own pace in a supportive environment, without stress and time pressures which are barriers to learning. A learning environment with the right mood and atmosphere is important.
- They need to be able to integrate prior knowledge and work experience to the new learning. When they return to their jobs they should be encouraged to apply the skills and knowledge learnt. The quicker they can do this the more effective the transfer of learning.
- Ideally they need to have developed 'learning how to learn' skills such as confidence, time management, presentation, mind maps, reading and memory skills.

## Risks/threats to the centre

The challenge of open learning is that many staff do not use it because of the pressing demands and deadlines during work time and they are often expected to use it during their own time without sufficient incentives. In practice, how do you encourage staff in such circumstances to use the corporate learning centre? The answer is, of course, you must provide them with the opportunity and time to use the centre as well as the encouragement and example, otherwise there is always the danger that the centre will become nothing more than an expensive 'corporate toy' or in a worse scenario a 'white elephant'. Even if open learning is used, evaluation is needed to assess its effectiveness and the extent to which the knowledge and skills are being transferred to the workplace.

## Summary

Force field analysis is a useful model for helping managers understand and resolve resistance to change. The decision maker uses the analysis to evaluate how the restraining forces can be removed or reduced and how the driving forces can be reinforced. Education, communication, participation and aggressive marketing are all ways of reducing or removing resistance from employees to open learning. Managers and trainers may also be unenthusiastic about the introduction of corporate learning centres. Management's lack of support, commitment and encouragement should be acknowledged and overcome. The idea of open learning may be seen as a threat by trainers and so they must be sold the idea and their support won.

# 6 Launching a corporate learning centre

## Introduction

Preparation and planning is the key to success in launching a corporate learning centre. The centre must be set up, fully equipped and furnished with good quality courseware and ready to go. The syllabus or guide to courses will have been printed and the initial marketing and advertising completed. The coordinator will have been appointed and trained in the requirements of the job. A good management information system will have been installed and tested so that booking and student records can be kept. The chief executive or local celebrity will have been booked to make the launch and the press invited to attend.

## Benchmarking

Before finally committing yourself you should visit a few companies who have successfully set up corporate learning centres. Find out at first hand what were the problems they encountered and how they overcame them. Ask how they went about organizing the launch, who they invited and so on. This information will prove invaluable. Benchmark your learning centre against the best you saw and plan to do even better.

## Networking PCs

In a large geographically dispersed organization you may be considering setting up several corporate learning centres. Using a local area network (LAN), PCs in the same building can be linked together. Similarly, PCs over a greater geographical area can be linked together using wide area networks (WANs). WANs are an obvious choice for companies with geographically dispersed regions or branch networks. Special telecommunications systems will be required and the cost of this must be compared to stand alone centres before a final decision is made. However, these networks have obvious advantages compared with stand alone centres. With the latter each centre will have to carry its own courseware. With networks the same courseware can be shared and should thus be more economical.

## Location

Corporate learning centres should be strategically located where there are high concentrations of employees and where they are easily accessible and highly visible. The best location is on the ground floor near the reception area and main entrance to the building. This gives maximum visibility and accessibility, especially for the disabled whose needs should be considered when designing the centre. Think about those employees who will be using the centre at night. It should be easy to find and the approach to the centre should be well lit and signposted. A location near the main entrance to the building will also encourage a high passing trade.

## Reception area

The reception area is used for counselling, course appraisal, administration, course enquiries and storage of learning materials, and generally for meeting customers and visitors. Ideally it should be designed to minimize disruption to other learners and to respect the privacy of learners. A quiet study atmosphere with minimum distraction is needed if learners are to concentrate and maintain self-discipline. A friendly and welcoming approach by the coordinator will create the right mood.

## Logo and signposting

Put up a large attractive sign on the door with the logo 'Walk in and help yourself to knowledge'. The door of the corporate learning centre should always be open. This is part of the policy of removing barriers to learning. The logo should be instantly recognizable as signifying a corporate learning centre. The creation of brand awareness and loyalty is an important goal. The logo should become synonymous with the centre.

# Layout and equipment

You will need a dedicated room for the corporate learning centre. See Figure 6.1 for a suggested layout. Ideally the room should be custom built but in reality this is often not the case and you must make do with the conversion of existing vacant office accommodation. The size of the room is determined by the number of booths for learners, reception area, coordinator's desk and display and storage facilities. Each booth is dedicated to a particular type of equipment and specific range of courseware. A laminated poster giving a general list of courses available in the booth may be displayed in a prominent place on the side of the booth. The individual workstations should provide comfort, seclusion and privacy for up to two learners or indeed for one learner with tutor support. Chairs should be ergonomically designed to prevent backache and maximize comfort. Tables should be of the appropriate height with plenty of surface space for working on.

The PCs in the booths should be linked up to a printer so that learners can print out their work if they wish. A colour printer might be considered for graphical packages such as Harvard Graphics, Freelance Graphics and Power Point. This facility has the added advantage of training learners in the use of printers.

## *Study booths*

The number, nature and layout of the study booths within the centre will depend on the following factors:

- number of customers expected to use the centre at any one time
- number of employees in the immediate catchment area
- shape and size of the room available
- furniture, equipment, media and courseware selected
- number of subjects catered for and their likely popularity
- budget allocated for setting up and equipping the centre
- particular needs of departments or locations.

In general terms, each booth should be supplied with:

- electrical and other sockets for equipment
- individual lighting if required
- adequate space for writing and course work
- shelving to temporarily store books, manuals or other user materials.

Figure 6.2 suggests how a nine-booth centre might be dedicated. Large centres may also have a booth for the teaching of corporate systems, with tutorials such as the personnel management information system, the management accounting and cost control system and the marketing

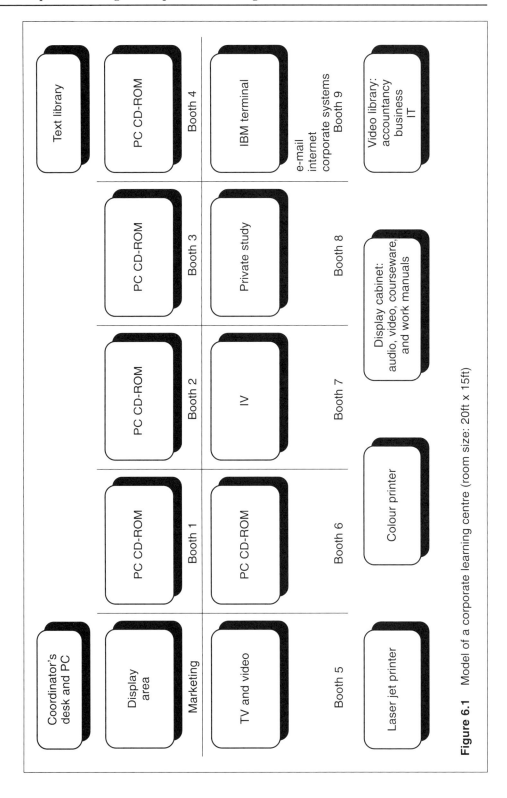

**Figure 6.1**    Model of a corporate learning centre (room size: 20ft x 15ft)

| Booth | Format | Subjects | Notes |
|---|---|---|---|
| 1 & 2 | CD-ROM | Keyboarding, wordprocessing, spreadsheets, graphics, general IT skills | Large demand for IT skills requires two dedicated booths |
| 3 | CD-ROM | Economics, management, marketing, financial accounting, costing, management accounting | Popular with staff studying formal qualifications |
| 4 | CD-ROM and CBT | Management and personal development | |
| 5 | TV and video | Accounting, finance, marketing, management, languages, IT | |
| 6 | Audio | Management and personal development | |
| 7 | Interactive video | Languages, IT, management, health and safety, technical, engineering | |
| 8 | Books, magazines etc. | Private study, reading and research | |
| 9 | Terminal | Corporate systems, e-mail and networks | Tutorials on PMIS, MOCCS, e-mail etc. |

**Figure 6.2**   Dedicated booths

information system. These systems may be on the mainframe with access from the corporate learning centre. This booth may also provide tutorials on e-mail.

Depending on the type of business, booths might also be dedicated to production, technical and engineering subjects. Health and safety is another topical area and for which there is courseware available. The subjects will depend on the needs of your particular business.

There should be a high standard of furnishing so that the centre is attractive to work in with sufficient equipment to accommodate the courseware.

## Coordinator's desk

The basic requirements for the coordinator will be a PC and a telephone. The PC should include software programmes with word-processing, desktop publishing, spreadsheet and graphical capabilities. These packages will be needed for marketing and advertising such as producing brochures, posters and a newsletter. The coordinator will also need e-mail and a good package for keeping training records of customers. E-mail is useful as a marketing and communications tool with customers inside and outside the organization.

## Text library

One display cabinet should be used for books and text-based programmes. Subject classification will be helpful to learners, as well as your own coding system to keep track of titles. Some subjects can go out of date quickly – make sure you stock the latest editions.

## Video library

Another display cabinet may be used for videos. These should also be kept in subject order and within subject by code order and displayed at eye level if possible.

## Audio library

This may be a separate display cabinet or may be shared with the text or video library. Special storage units can be purchased for audiotapes. They should be kept by subject and within subject by code order.

*General display cabinet*

CBT, CD-ROM and IV packages and the associated workbooks and documentation may be stored in a general display cabinet. Display cabinets should be attractive and organized so that users can see the contents clearly and, if possible, at eye level. Depending on the size and variety of courses stocked it might be a good idea to organize them by subject area or by media, for example, books, audio, video and computer courseware, and within the media classification by subject area. Each item should have a learning centre code number. However, whatever the classification system it should be user friendly. Courseware starts to become out of date as soon as it is made and should be kept under constant review both for physical condition and relevancy.

*General information stand*

Provision should be made for a general information stand to display the corporate learning centre catalogue, users' guide to courses, health and welfare literature, college brochures offering part-time courses and new and popular open learning programmes. Corporate videos such as those on the annual report and accounts, strategic plan or safety could also be displayed. This type of sales promotion can generate interest and business from people who just 'pop in' out of curiosity to see what the corporate learning centre is all about. It is a focal and talking point and gives the coordinator an opportunity to engage the client in conversation about courses on offer and to sell the centre.

## The learning environment

A corporate learning centre must be a comfortable and pleasant place for working in. Further design considerations should include:

- adequate toilet and drinking water facilities nearby
- heating, lighting and ventilation of a high standard with minimum noise disturbance
- lighting positioned in such a way that it does not shine directly onto the computer screens
- window blinds may be needed to prevent sunlight shining onto computer screens
- air conditioning
- VDUs fitted with anti-glare protection screens
- health and safety legislation.

State-of-the-art decor and equipment will look professional. The room should be soundproofed, carpeted and brightly painted with colourful pictures on the walls. Warm colours create the right ambience for learning. The pictures should have a relaxing, learning and educational theme. Suppliers' posters may be suitable and these should be framed. Plants strategically situated around the room will add to the atmosphere of peace, learning and relaxation. Every effort should be made to make the environment conducive to learning and non-threatening.

Soft classical baroque music is reputed to enhance learning effectiveness and memory and may be played in the background. It has a rhythm of one beat per second or 60 beats per minute. Users of corporate learning centres where this background music is played confirm that they find it enjoyable, relaxing and conducive to learning.

## Technical support

Technical support may be provided within the organization or from outside. There are companies that will lease the hardware, supply the software and provide technical support all in one package. There is no doubt that problems will arise from time to time with hardware and software and technical support must be available quickly to solve them.

The coordinator must be trained to diagnose and solve routine problems. A booklet on routine maintenance and trouble shooting would be a useful reference. Thus the coordinator should have good knowledge of PCs, associated equipment and operating systems. Technical support for software is often provided by the suppliers. However, problems associated with hardware should be left to the experts.

In practice modern technology is becoming more reliable. Nevertheless when there are problems it's essential that help is quickly at hand, therefore whoever gets the maintenance contract must be fast, efficient and reliable. There is nothing more frustrating from a user's point of view than having learning appointments cancelled because of malfunctioning hardware and software. From the coordinator's viewpoint the loss of business may be difficult to make up.

## Why establish a centre?

Market research should be carried out to establish the likely demand for a corporate learning centre. Research could take the form of face-to-face or telephone interviews using a questionnaire.

## Piloting

Where a number of corporate learning centres are to be set up in the organization it might be a good idea to run a pilot centre initially to test out the concept. If it works then the other centres could be opened up gradually. The advantage of this approach is that you can learn from mistakes made and take corrective action in subsequent centres.

# Pre-launch planning

If the market research is favourable then after the centre has been set up the official launch may be planned. Before the official launch the organization should carry out a major communications and marketing drive to increase staff awareness of the purpose and concept of corporate learning centres, the advantages of open learning, the location of the centre, the type of media used, and the duration and range of courses stocked. Now is the opportunity to sell the benefits of the centre to:

- employees (and overcome their resistance)
- managers (and overcome their resistance)
- directors (and win their support)
- reinforce the organization's commitment to individual development, to learning and the achievement of corporate objectives
- reinforce the importance of the centre in the eyes of the employees, by chief executive and director level participation and the involvement of external dignitaries (the local mayor if you wanted to use the centre to highlight the organization's importance to the local community, or other appropriate 'celebrities' if you wanted to suggest that learning is 'OK').

A chart of the corporate learning centre project plan is shown in Figure 6.3.

## Selling to managers

Talk to as many managers and staff in your organization as possible and let them know about the forthcoming launch of the corporate learning centre and the facilities that will be available.

## Course syllabus

Distribute a syllabus, 'A guide to corporate learning centre courses', to every employee in your organization. The syllabus should be user friendly and up to date, listing under subject areas all the courses available in the corporate learning centre. It should also contain an introduction to the concept of open learning and give instructions on booking a course and the centre's exact location.

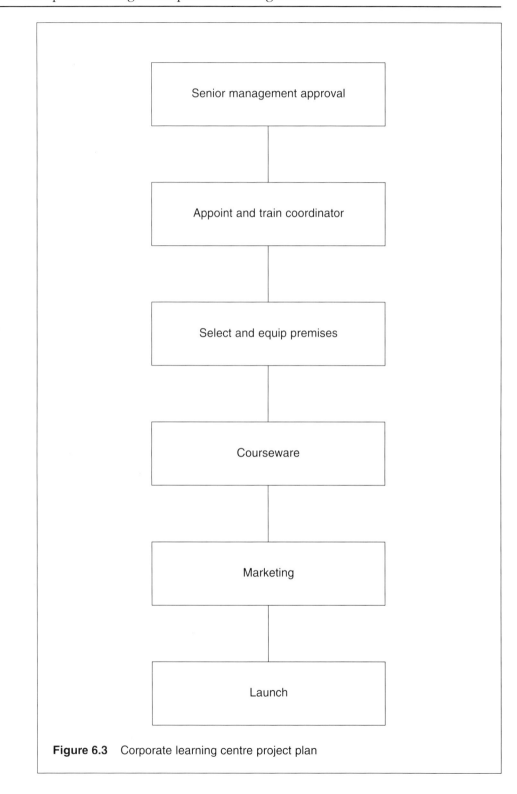

**Figure 6.3**   Corporate learning centre project plan

## Course catalogue

A more comprehensive course catalogue should be prepared for managers for reference. Each course is allocated a page in the catalogue giving subject group, course code, title, learning objectives, content, duration, delivery system and equipment required for the courseware.

## Public relations

Write an article about the launch of the centre for your local newspaper and the company newsletter. Local radio stations should also be informed about the event. Specialist computer and educational magazines could be targeted. The idea is to create as much publicity and interest in the corporate learning centre as possible. This is also very good publicity generally for your company, particularly as a provider of state-of-the-art training and development procedures.

# Official launch

The chief executive of your organization will carry out the official launch and give an address on the mission and role of corporate learning centres in training and development and their contribution to corporate objectives and the personal development of individuals. This address should be followed by a reception with wine and refreshments. Guided tours of the centre and demonstrations of courseware may be provided for those interested in seeing the facilities available.

## Sales promotion during the launch

Use the launch as an opportunity for an in-house sales promotion campaign, using notice boards, e-mail, in-house journals such as company and departmental newsletters, posters and the internal postal system to distribute newsletters and brochures.

## Presentations

Live presentations on corporate learning centres will arouse the interest of departments, work stations, participation councils and interested employees. Employees will not just flock into the corporate learning centre when it opens. They must be made aware of how they will benefit from open learning. They must be educated. They have to be told that it exists, where it is located, what services it provides and the benefits of using those services. All this must be communicated to each employee by good advertising.

## *External use*

Guided tours around the corporate learning centre should be available for groups from inside and outside the organization on request. As soon as the novelty wears off numbers using the centre are bound to fall. It might be a good idea to open the centre's facilities to children and relatives of staff and outside companies on a fee-paying basis to keep the capacity of the centre fully occupied. Small organizations who do not have the resources themselves to finance a corporate learning centre may like to use its services. Clarify any copyright issues on the centre's courseware with the original producer before you do this.

## *Marketing before and after the launch*

Marketing must be on a continuous basis to maintain custom and interest. If you don't market the corporate learning centre it will become under-utilized and the expensive equipment will slowly gather dust.

## Corporate learning centre newsletter

Interest is renewed through advertising and sales promotion in a corporate learning centre newsletter on a monthly or bimonthly basis. Brochures and e-mail may also be used to advise of new courses and to target particular individuals and categories of employees.

The company newsletter can highlight success stories about employees who have completed corporate learning centre programmes, their feedback on the programme and how they applied it to their work. People like to be treated as winners and this type of publicity will encourage further bookings.

The newsletter may be produced cheaply in-house by the coordinator using a desktop publishing package. Contents may include reviews of new and popular courses, tips on learning skills and advances in education technology. The internal noticeboard could be used for special promotional displays, but a special corporate learning centre noticeboard placed at strategic locations throughout the company is probably the best option as there is often fierce competition from other departments for space on internal noticeboards

## Summary

Corporate learning centres should be located where there are high concentrations of employees and where they are easily accessible and highly visible. A reception area is needed for counselling, course appraisal, administration, course enquiries and storage of learning materials. The booths may be dedicated to particular equipment and specified subject courseware. The environment should offer the right mood and atmosphere for learners.

Market research is carried out to establish the likely demand for a corporate learning centre. If this is favourable then an official launch can be planned and implemented. An in-house sales promotion campaign should be undertaken using noticeboards, e-mail, in-house journals and posters. Marketing is not only needed at the launch stage but also on a continuous basis to maintain custom and interest. An up-to-date catalogue of corporate learning centre courseware is necessary. Technical support is essential if the centre is to run smoothly. A trained coordinator will be able to diagnose and solve routine problems.

# 7  The media used in a corporate learning centre

## Introduction

The media used in corporate learning centres include computer-based training, interactive video, CD-ROM, CD-interactive, audio, video, the Internet, e-mail, and of course books and workbooks. They will be described and their advantages and limitations discussed.

## Computer-based training (CBT)

Computer-based training is one of the most cost effective training media. It is an interactive learning experience between the learner and the computer in which the computer provides most of the stimulus, the learner responds, and the computer then analyses the response and provides learner feedback. In other words, the material should be user friendly, interactive and provide knowledge of results. Its physical form is a 3.5" disk.

PCs have improved greatly in recent years and CBT courses are now of a high standard with clear learning objectives, colour, graphics, high interaction and some animation. A few years ago they were literally books on disks with the minimum of interaction.

The one-to-one nature of CBT enables constant monitoring of learner understanding. A well designed programme will respond immediately to the needs of the individual learner and will maintain a log of progress. CBT courseware is inexpensive to reproduce and distribute. In a hierarchy of cost CBT is the cheapest, CD-ROM is much more expensive and IV is more expensive still. CBT has been used successfully in large banks and building societies to teach employees basic business and banking procedures. However, it lacks the realism and immediacy of television which is sometimes useful for interpersonal skills training and which is a feature of IV. Figure 7.1 shows a comparative chart of the media used in corporate learning centres. There is a good range of CBT courseware in most areas of training.

## Interactive video (IV)

Interactive video has many of the advantages of live training such as hearing, seeing and interacting, with the added advantage that a consistent message is conveyed each time – it is not subject to bad days on the part of the trainer. IV has proved to be effective for people learning basic language skills such as French and German. Some of the programmes use touch screen technology instead of keyboard input, making them extremely user friendly.

IV has also proved popular with staff eager to familiarize themselves with the fundamentals of computing and PC skills by the use of 'touch screen technology', an aid to those who lack keyboarding skills. Because of the high degree of interactivity IV has proved very good at training people in interpersonal relationship skills such as interviewing, communicating and presentation. The IV player uses video disks (in appearance like the traditional vinyl long-playing record with the addition of vision). So the IV player linked to a PC produces sound and vision just like your TV set but, unlike the TV, it is an interactive learning media. In some corporate learning centres IV has proved disappointing mainly because the computer hardware is perceived as too cumbersome to use for some programmes.

## Compact disk – read only memory (CD-ROM)

The CD-ROM multimedia courses are generally rated very highly by users. It looks exactly like the CD disk you have in your home stereo but is formatted for computer data rather than sound. It is the cheapest form of storage device with the capacity of about 500 floppy disks. You can store about 250,000 pages on it, which is the equivalent of 500 books. CD-ROM provides access to very large information banks, with text, colour, graphics, high quality still images and some moving pictures with high quality sound.

The CD-ROM player may be a separate unit, but is more likely to be a built-in feature of the modern PC. This demonstrates the confidence that the computer industry has in the future of the CD-ROM. The term multimedia is now taken to mean the CD-ROM as the delivery mechanism. Interactive video instruction (IV) is another example of

| Media | Strengths | Weaknesses | Subjects | Ability to hold interest |
|---|---|---|---|---|
| CBT | Inexpensive<br>Interaction<br>Feedback | Limited movement<br>No sound<br>Limited images<br>Lacks realism of TV | Most topics | Good |
| IV | Images<br>Sound<br>TV quality<br>Interaction | Expensive hardware<br>Expensive software | Computers<br>Management<br>Languages<br>Interpersonal skills | Excellent |
| CD-ROM | Images<br>Sound<br>Large capacity | More expensive than CBT | Increasing range available | Very Good |
| Audio | Flexible<br>Inexpensive | No images<br>Passive<br>No feedback | Most topics<br>Management audios | Poor |
| Video | Images<br>Sound | Passive<br>No feedback | All topics | Good |
| Text | Portable<br>Inexpensive | Little interaction | All topics | Poor |

**Figure 7.1**   Media used in corporate learning centres

multimedia courseware. In fact any courseware that combines text with sound and pictures could be considered multimedia.

CD-ROM training courseware is available for Microsoft Office, Word Perfect, Power Point and Microsoft Word, as well as introductions to PCs and computing. Human resource development skills are also covered on CD-ROM with programmes on leadership, motivation, time management, presentation and writing. Operational management skills such as statistical process control and total quality management are also catered for.

## *Education*

There is now a new range of software in the area of education which blends the advanced graphics and slick presentation of top selling games with solid educational experiences. They are known as 'Edutainment' packages and cover many subjects. They are aimed at children aged four years and up. Examples include Microsoft's Encarta and Microsoft's Musical Instruments. Encarta is a complete encyclopedia on CD-ROM. Its great advantage over conventional encyclopedias is that it combines sound, text, graphics and video which, of course, adds to its overall appeal and educational value. Microsoft's Musical Instruments has topics ranging from accordion to zurna and is divided into four broad sections – families of instruments, instruments of the world, an A to Z of instruments and music ensembles. These are discovery learning packages which put fun back into learning, where it should be. There are also CD-ROM packages on history, geography, the human body and other educational topics.

Because of its vastly superior capabilities it is very likely that in the future CD-ROM will supersede CBT and IV as the leading courseware medium in corporate learning centres. Modern PCs include a CD-ROM drive as a standard feature.

## Compact Disk – Interactive (CDI)

The Compact Disk-Interactive is a multimedia system based on the compact disk and was launched in the early 1990s by Philips. It can include high quality pictures, graphics, text and sound and needs a CDI player linked to a television set. Dryden and Vos (1994) report that the Smithsonian Institute in Washington DC has compressed displays of history, technology, science, space and art on one CDI – an interactive compact video disk, ready for instant replay on any television screen.

Encyclopedias with pictures, text and a sound track can now be put onto one interactive video disk which can be played through a television screen. Soon it will be possible to dial up that information from a worldwide database and have it played on individual interactive television sets. The entire works of your favourite writers could be made instantly available to you when you want it. CDI is still to make its entry into corporate learning centres and its future in this area is uncertain. The lack of software packages for this medium is still a problem. It has failed to catch the imagination of the buying public as much as the CD-ROM.

# Audiotapes

Audiotapes have proved quite popular with corporate learning centre users. Many learners use the loan service and listen to tapes at home in their own time. They can also be listened to in the car while commuting to and from work and because of this have proved very popular. Why not use this time to increase your education in management, personal development, languages and so on? Think of all the subject areas you could become expert in if you used your journey time productively. Many people spend up to two hours or more each day commuting to and from work – about 10 hours a week, or up to 460 hours per typical working year. In a few years you could study the equivalent of a university degree programme while commuting to work, in your car or by public transport.

You can listen as often as you like and replay the material as often as you like. You can stop the tape anywhere you wish and repeat any parts until you really understand the points. In a lecture situation it is not possible to do this. Audiotapes are very good for learners who are not too fond of reading.

Some people find it difficult to concentrate for long periods of time on the spoken word. This can be overcome to a certain extent by stopping the cassette player every ten minutes or so and summarizing key points to date. Better still, create a Mind Map of the tape as you listen. At the end you will have a comprehensive Mind Map completed which you can use to review the topic in the future. Some audio programmes come complete with workbooks, exercises and projects to provide the necessary amount of interaction to help learning.

# Videotapes

A picture speaks more than a thousand words and moving pictures with sound add an extra dimension. Many videotape programmes are accompanied by workbooks which facilitate interaction with the material. Video programmes are particularly suitable for language training and there is a wide range of these available.

There are a good variety of suppliers who produce high quality management videos aimed at supervisory, management and professional people. There is also a wide range of videos on information technology and other technical subjects.

## Internet and e-mail

The Internet is a labyrinth of academic, commercial, government and military computer networks that are interconnected. It was started in 1969 as an experimental network by the US Department of Defence. One of its original objectives was to enable scientists working on government grants to communicate with each other.

The experiment started by connecting four computers. Now the Internet connects more than 45,000 computer networks in government, education, business, military and consumer areas, in more than 70 countries. Each network can support from a few to thousands of users. The Internet is now a network of 30 million computer users with links to leading educational establishments throughout the world.

Access to the Internet would provide a useful resource to second- and third-level students. It suggests all sorts of possibilities, especially for distance learning. The technology is now there which will enable learners in different organizations anywhere in the world to link up with each other and share knowledge and experience. Multinational companies, for example, will have learners from different countries following the same course and supported by the same tutor with whom they can communicate via e-mail. The global village is now on our doorsteps.

E-mail is one of the most widely used features of the internet. Large businesses have used e-mail for years, enabling employees to send messages, memos and reports to each other. But in the past most systems only worked within single organizations. The advantage of linking into the Internet is that you can now send e-mail to other organizations. E-mail can be used to market the corporate learning centre not only to your own employees but to outside businesses as well.

Littlefield (1994) reports that Edinburgh's Telford College is developing innovative forms of open learning using e-mail. It uses this medium to run a course for students in Denmark who are studying for a Scottish vocational qualification in communication studies. They are also looking for EU funding to run an English language course for people in remote parts of Europe where they can communicate with Edinburgh using British Telecom's new £3,000 PC-based videophone.

## Text-based courses

With all the emphasis on technology, we should not forget the humble book. Bates (1988) says that while technology can bring many benefits to open learning, in most cases it is not a cheap option, and needs to be used with care and skill. For this reason, established media such as print have an important role to play in open learning. Indeed books have most of the advantages of computer-based training, such as accessibility and flexibility, without the cost of expensive hardware and software and have the added advantage of being very portable. In fact much courseware is accompanied by manuals. Books, like courseware, provide content expertise. Courseware is usually more attractive and easier to learn. But books can also be made user friendly.

With the greater awareness of learning theory, and the arrival of desktop publishing, the quality, design and layout of books has improved dramatically in the last few years. Chapters often start with learning objectives and overviews and conclude with summaries – the old 'tell 'em what you're going to tell 'em, and then tell 'em what you've told 'em' principle put into practice. The design, quality of illustrations, layout and typography has also advanced considerably. So nowadays, books because they are well written are easier to read and understand.

## Magazines and journals

The corporate learning centre should stock a suitable range of magazines and journals aimed at the learners. The type of magazines will be determined by the type of employees the centre services. A typical range might include management, marketing, business, accountancy, information technology and technical and engineering journals.

## Summary

CBT is one of the most cost effective training media. It is an interactive learning experience between a learner and a computer in which the computer provides the majority of the stimulus, the learner responds, and the computer analyses the response and provides learner feedback. IV has many of the advantages of live training such as hearing, seeing and interacting. Some of the programmes use touch screen technology instead of keyboard input, making them extremely user friendly. CD-ROM multimedia courses are generally rated very highly by users. CD-ROM disks look exactly like the CD disk in your home stereo but are formatted for computer data rather than sound.

CDI has high quality pictures, graphics, text and sound and needs a CDI player linked up to a television set. It is now possible to put encyclopedias with pictures, text and a soundtrack on one interactive video disk which can be played through a television. Audiotapes are very popular with corporate learning centre users as they can be listened to in learners' own time and while commuting to and from work. Videotapes are popular because they can be viewed at home.

Organizations can be connected to each other by using the Internet. With all the emphasis on technology the humble book should not be forgotten. It can still play an important role in any corporate learning centre.

# 8 Management and administration

## Introduction

This chapter examines the role of the coordinator and the administration and management of a corporate learning centre. Housekeeping, security, administration, health and safety and the role of the coordinator as tutor will be explored. The need for the support of mentors will also be discussed.

## Organization

The organization of a corporate learning centre can range from a centralized to a decentralized structure. Centralization offers economies of scale but may become bureaucratic and inflexible. Decentralization encourages initiative and flexibility but may incur some duplication of resources.

The best organization structure centre depends on the circumstances in the company. Even with decentralization and corporate learning centres under the control of local management it will still be necessary to have a strong functional influence from the training and development department.

Questions of mission, policy, finance and budgets, design and location, purchase of courseware and equipment, staffing and administration, management and reporting arrangements have all to be thought out very clearly. Logistical, tactical and strategic plans should be drawn up and linked to the training and development plan and ultimately to the formal corporate planning process of the company. Planning and control are known as the Siamese twins of management. So planning presumes objectives, targets and budgets, and control is the comparison of actual results against targets and the taking of corrective action to put the actual activities of the corporate learning centre back on target again.

## Coordinator's person specification

A corporate learning centre coordinator is likely to possess all round skills:

- able to work intensively for long periods under demanding conditions
- good appearance
- recognised qualification in information technology
- experience in training and open learning
- good problem-solving and diagnostic skills
- good customer relations
- good telephone voice and manner
- good administration
- selling and marketing skills
- good hands-on information technology skills
- desktop publishing, graphical and spreadsheet skills
- interested in keeping up to date with computer-based training
- a self developer
- training and development
- solving learning needs of employees
- self-starter
- capable of accepting responsibility
- able to handle demands of customers simultaneously
- capable of withstanding pressure
- friendly and extrovert
- willing to work overtime, if necessary.

In general coordinators must have a good personality and an interest in training and development and the learning needs of employees. They must enjoy meeting people and solving their training needs. Listening, empathizing, counselling and tutoring skills are all necessary for the job. They must have a sympathetic ear for the concerns and problems of employees. Fricker (1988) says that Austin Rover has a corporate learning centre at each of its manufacturing plants. These are staffed by an administrator (normally a training officer) whose principal role is to help the learners 'help themselves' and steer them through the learning packages.

# Coordinator's job description

The coordinator's job will comprise the following skills:

- day-to-day administration and management of the corporate learning centre
- promote and market corporate learning centre courseware
- operate the management information system
- liaise with suppliers of hardware and software
- draw and agree the budget for the centre
- generally assist learners as necessary
- operate and control the home loan library system for audios, videos and text
- ensure that the centre is kept tidy and clean
- ensure that copyright is not infringed
- maintain stationery stocks for the centre
- select and purchase courseware and equipment
- certify invoices and pass to accounts for payment
- devise and agree costing and pricing systems
- keep up to date on computer-based training
- code new items and keep the catalogue and course syllabus up to date
- issue a quarterly corporate learning centre newsletter
- show visitors around the centre
- carry out a virus security check each morning
- have hands-on familiarity with the main courseware
- carry out routine problem solving and equipment maintenance
- make sure that learners fill up evaluation of courseware forms on completion of courses
- maintain contact with managers regarding their requirements for corporate learning courses
- carry out occasional surveys to get feedback from users on the quality of corporate learning centre courses and service
- produce statistics on usage of the centre as required.

Coordinators must be familiar with the main courseware stocked in the corporate learning centre. They can use any spare time to acquire this expertise. They could also advise on the content, standard and duration of the programme. Coordinators cannot be subject experts on everything but over a period of time they can acquire expertise in many areas by studying subject courseware for which there is a good demand. However, they may recommend subject experts or specialists elsewhere in the organization.

# Course guide

The coordinator must ensure that the course guide is kept up to date. Each course is recorded under four headings: code number, title, type (audio, video, text, CBT, CD-ROM or IV) and duration in hours. New courses need to be added and old courses, and those no longer in demand, should be withdrawn. Updates or reprints of the guide should be carried out annually.

## Computer security and virus protection

The coordinator will switch on the computers each morning and operate the virus checking software. A virus could be introduced into the system by learners using disks from outside. It is important that this risk is safeguarded against and that the integrity of the system is maintained. The virus checking software must be kept up to date. To prevent contamination by virus, software should not be loaned out from the centre. CBT, CD-ROM and IV courses should be studied in the centre only under the supervision of the coordinator.

## Copyright

Computer software is protected by copyright law and, to a lesser extent, by patent law. Copyright protects the expression of the idea but not the idea itself. The form is protected and not the idea. The reproduction of a programme is an infringement of the rightholder's copyright. This applies to print, video, audio, illustrations, photographs, computer software and broadcast programmes. There are some legal concessions for education and training if the material is used in-house and not for commercial gain. However, always obtain copyright permission if you want to reproduce illustrations.

Unauthorized copying of software, audio or video programmes is illegal unless the user has permission or a licence to do so. A company may be liable for damages if its employees infringe copyright. Apart from the vigilance of the coordinator, periodic checks by the company's internal auditors will act as a deterrent.

The corporate learning centre coordinator must not allow breach of copyright. Learners should not be allowed to copy materials in the learning centre for their private use. It might also be the policy of the centre not to loan disks or videos to learners in case of breach of copyright or introduction of viruses into the system. A licence may be obtained from the owner to make multiple copies of a programme if the company feel there is a demand. Many software and video programmes are now protected to prevent unauthorized copying. If in doubt, always consult the original producer of the material.

# Bookings and preparation

The coordinator will review bookings for the day, enter them on the PC programme and record bookings that have been taken up on the previous day. Learners should be advised to book in advance as they may be disappointed if they just turn up on the day and the particular booth is already booked. Likewise they should also give adequate notice of cancellations so that other learners are not prevented from using the booth at that time. A strict policy must be operated in this regard. Learners who fail to give advance notice of cancellations should be reminded that this is unacceptable. Courseware should be preloaded on the machines and be menu driven so that everything is ready for the learner on arrival.

# Information and feedback

At the start of each week the coordinator should provide information to the management on usage of the corporate learning centre for the previous week. This information will identify who is using the centre and the type of courses that are in high demand. In the case of multisites, comparative usage statistics should be given. An inter-centre league table could be compiled and the reason for differences investigated.

Course evaluation sheets should be issued to learners and completed evaluation forms returned to the coordinator before the learner leaves the centre. This feedback will help validate courses for quality, relevance, user friendliness, design and timeliness (up to date). Courses with consistently poor feedback should be withdrawn and replaced with better quality programmes. This feedback, where relevant, may also be supplied to producers to help them upgrade their courses.

# Stock management

Keep a record of all issues and returns of books, audios and videos. Where a personal and postal loan system is in operation a vigorous follow-up system will ensure that loaned material is returned promptly and will prevent other clients waiting unnecessarily. It may be the policy of the corporate learning centre to insist that clients must replace lost items but this rule should be applied with discretion. An up-to-date inventory of books, audios and videos will ensure that all stock is accounted for.

# Courseware acquisition

The coordinator may be responsible for purchase and screening of courseware. Courseware may date quickly or suffer damage through repeated use and so should be upgraded or replaced as necessary. This may be carried out in conjunction with subject experts and the training and development department who should ensure adherence to corporate training policy and avoid duplication of effort and overlap. There must be good reasons for booking employees onto external courses if the equivalent course is available in the corporate learning centre.

## Equipment purchase and maintenance

An experienced coordinator should be able to make most purchasing decisions without recourse to third parties. Large companies with many corporate learning centres may employ specialist staff for the purchase of courseware. Equipment must be maintained, upgraded and replaced. Maintenance contracts can be placed with equipment suppliers. They must be able to offer a helpline for routine problems and respond quickly when equipment breaks down.

## Personal skills

The coordinator must have a friendly and helpful telephone manner. Bookings may be made in person or on the phone and the coordinator should build up a good relationship with clients. Being friendly, listening with empathy, remembering and using clients' names are important skills for the coordinator to develop. As well as attracting new customers they have to build and maintain loyalty amongst existing customers.

## Absence

An important aspect of administration is providing for relief when the coordinator is on holiday, sick leave or attending a training course. Most of this absence can be planned for with the exception of sick leave and cover must be provided. The 'relief' must be trained to take over the duties of the coordinator smoothly and should be available at short notice in case of emergencies.

## Housekeeping

The coordinator will organize the cleaners so that the corporate learning centre is part of their daily roster. The coordinator should also ensure that the centre is tidy and that computer keyboards and screens, headphones and disks are kept clean. The head on the video recorder must always be clean. For hygiene reasons headphones should be disinfected occasionally to guard against the possibility of ear infections.

# Security

Security and control are an important aspect of the coordinator's job. Courseware should be kept under lock and key and issued under the control and watchful eye of the coordinator to prevent unauthorized tampering and copying. Remember, the company is responsible for employee infringement of copyright. An inventory of courseware and hardware should be made on a regular basis to ensure that everything is controlled and accounted for. An inventory of hardware may be displayed on the wall of the corporate learning centre. The items stocked in the centre are valuable and easily transportable and should be protected from theft or damage.

The corporate learning centre should be staffed at all times during the day. At other times, access should only be to authorized staff with the swipe card or similar security. All software packages including videos, audios and books, should be locked in glass display cabinets and under the control of the coordinator.

# Data protection

All organizations which store data on individuals should be aware of their legal duties. Under the Data Protection Act individuals have a right to know who is keeping information about them on computer files. They are entitled to be told the purpose for and the type of information held. Computer users must comply with a series of data protection principles, which include acquiring data 'fairly' and keeping it accurate and up to date. Personal data should be adequate, relevant and not excessive for its purpose and should be secured against unauthorized access.

# Health and safety

The coordinator has general responsibility for the health and safety of clients while they are using the learning centre. Potential dangers include trailing wires, unsecured bookshelves, slippery floors, courseware left on passageways and so on. Good housekeeping and tidiness will prevent many dangers from arising. Static electricity may be a problem where there are screens and carpets in a confined area. Antistatic sprays can deal with the problem.

The coordinator should be aware of potential health problems caused by prolonged use of VDUs some of which relate to matters of safety. Symptoms include headaches, backaches, sore finger joints, fatigue and tired eyes. Further information is available in a leaflet entitled 'Working with VDUs' issued by the UK Health and Safety Executive.

Continuous working in front of a VDU may cause fatigue. The coordinator should advise learners to take frequent breaks every half hour or so. There have been several studies on whether working with a VDU can affect an operator's eyesight. None of them has found any evidence to link VDUs with damage to the eyes or to make existing eye defects worse. In any event all the VDUs in the corporate learning centre should be fitted with a protection screen to cut down on glare.

The coordinator should ensure that learners are comfortably seated and that the learning centre is well lit and quiet to minimize the risk of headaches, backaches or eye strain. The chairs should have adjustable height and back support and the desks should be of an appropriate height. Good posture will help prevent backache, muscle tiredness and discomfort in the arms, shoulders and neck.

Modern systems have detachable keyboards and adjustable tilt swivel screens which may be positioned to suit individual needs. It is not advisable for clients to rest their wrists on the edge of the keyboard or desk or bend their hands up at the wrist. They should try to keep a soft touch on the keys and not over-stretch their fingers. Good keyboard technique is important in prolonged operation.

Encourage learners to experiment with different layouts of keyboard, screen and document holder to find the best arrangement. Desks should be arranged so that any bright lights are not reflected on the screen. Learners should not look directly at windows or bright lights. Use curtains or blinds to cut out unwanted light.

# Training needs

An ongoing aspect of the coordinator's role is that of tutor, counsellor, facilitator and training needs advisor. Many people will visit the corporate learning centre without any clear idea of their training needs or what courses they want to do. Through a process of listening and questioning the coordinator will try to identify their training needs and endeavour to match an open learning course to meet those needs. The client should agree the outcome of the course with their immediate supervisor or manager to ensure their support.

The rationale behind a client's choice of course might include:

● to upgrade or learn a new skill
● to prepare for a new job or help promotion prospects
● to train in new information technology
● personal interest
● to supplement studies for a formal professional or university degree
● to revise a subject area or prepare for a 'live' training programme.

# Learning styles

In matching the course to the client the coordinator must consider not only the client's needs but also learning style. Some people are interested in theories and concepts while others are more interested in the practical application of ideas. Learners may be either left brain dominant or right brain dominant. This means that some may be analytical and rational and prefer logical and sequential learning experiences whilst others may be creative and artistic and enjoy plenty of interaction and visual learning experiences.

Does the learner prefer listening, seeing or activity? Do they enjoy learning holistically by considering overviews and broad concepts, or logically by sequentially working through details? Courses that cater for a combination of these styles will be most effective. This consideration may suggest the most suitable medium for the learner – text, audio, video, CBT, IV or CD-ROM. The coordinator should encourage learners to match the complexity of courseware to their experience.

# Welcoming new learners

Some learners require more help than others, perhaps in drawing up learning objectives, a training plan and time schedule to meet their needs. Learners are unlikely to be as familiar as the coordinator with the type, range and duration of the courses available in the corporate learning centre, so the coordinator must share expertise with learners. A mix of courses may be needed to meet particular training needs. The coordinator must be supportive rather than intrusive. Too much interference can overwhelm new learners. Shy learners may need help but be unwilling to ask. The coordinator must learn when to offer help and advice and when to stay in the background.

New learners are likely to need more support than experienced learners. Empathy, understanding, patience and a little humour is needed on the part of the tutor. A brief explanation as to how computers work and a quick introduction to the keyboard may be needed. Some people may have difficulty in operating the mouse. A little instruction in its use will help overcome their initial awkwardness and develop the right sensitivity of touch to use the mouse proficiently. The coordinator may give an initial demonstration on how to switch on and close down the computers; how to load the CD-ROM drive; how to access relevant courseware and how to move around the screen. This will help ensure that new learners make the most from their time.

Encourage new learners to use demonstrations or tutorials before they tackle the courseware and to take the keyboarding skills course and the introduction to PCs and DOS course. A lot of courseware is now Windows-based, and Microsoft's introductory and advanced CD-ROM courses on Windows should be recommended to new learners.

## The learning curve

Employees will go through a learning curve. In any new learning situation there is an initial stage of rapid progress, a stage of slow progress and a stage when little or no progress is made. This last stage is called the learning plateau and is the point when many learners become discouraged and give up. Seemingly insurmountable problems present themselves which will only be overcome if the learner sticks to the task. This stage may prove a real test of the learner's confidence and commitment, but once overcome the learner can progress to a higher level of expertise. During the plateau stage the advice, support, encouragement and counselling of the tutor is most important.

## More experienced learners

As learners use the corporate learning centre, so they become more confident and competent and will require less support. These self-sufficient learners should be encouraged to walk in and help themselves to learning and may act as useful advocates of the centre among new employees.

## Mentor support

Mentor support is a useful aid to developing open learning. The role of the mentor is to advise, coach, coax, encourage, support, empathize with and generally assist learners. Mentors might be fellow learners, colleagues, supervisors or managers. Mentoring compensates somewhat for the problem of isolation inherent in open learning by providing human contact and a source of support and advice when needed. The decision to accept a mentor or access a mentor should rest entirely with the individuals concerned.

Irrespective of the effectiveness of self-assessment questions and exercises within courseware, they are no substitute for face-to-face feedback. Mentoring offers an opportunity to build up lasting relationships with others in the company which may be helpful to career development in the future.

Learners who have recently completed the course may also be willing to act as mentors. They have the advantage of knowing the problems, pitfalls and anxieties of the course. The coordinator may act as a go-between to place new learners with appropriate mentors.

Meetings with mentors can be formal or informal. In a formal situation a timetable of meetings may be agreed. In an informal situation, especially in smaller companies, people might just occasionally bump into each other in the corridor. These impromptu meetings may then be turned into opportunities for the mentor to find out how the learner is progressing and to offer some advice and words of encouragement. This may be all the learner needs to stick to the task. The company may also consider running workshops for people who are interested in taking on the role of mentors. These workshops explain the purpose of mentoring, how people learn and the common problems experienced by learners.

A learning agreement between mentor and learner will set out what each expects of the other with a timetable of objectives and outcomes. Where the mentor is the supervisor or manager the mentoring process may be linked to individual training plans. This helps integrate the service provided by the corporate learning centre into the work of the company.

# Study groups

Corporate learning centre users may also form study groups to meet occasionally and exchange knowledge, skills and experiences. This can be a great way of learning, getting support and making friends. Study groups will help counteract the isolation of open learning and at the same time help members develop interpersonal skills.

# Summary

The ideal coordinator to run a corporate learning centre will have a certificate in information technology, a good personality with customer relations skills and an interest in education, training and development. Administration includes maintaining a course catalogue and operating a booking procedure for courses during the day. A good software package is necessary to facilitate this process. Course evaluation should be on an ongoing basis. The coordinator may be responsible for purchase and screening of courseware.

The co-ordinator should ensure that the centre is kept tidy and that computer keyboards and screens, headphones and disks are clean. Security and control are an important aspect of the job. The centre must be marketed creatively and continuously.

An important aspect of the coordinator's role is that of tutor, counsellor, facilitator and training needs advisor. The coordinator should suit the course to the learner's needs. The learner's preferred learning style should be a consideration. In an ideal situation, mentor support would be a feature of open learning. Mentoring is particularly necessary for the younger employee or for the new employee in the company.

# 9   Marketing the corporate learning centre

## Introduction

To survive in the long term the centre must be marketed creatively and on an ongoing basis. A good coordinator will be able to advise the learner of the pros and cons of various courses and media. This is an important marketing aspect of the coordinator's job and one of the ways in which new customers are identified and developed and new programmes purchased to meet the needs of learners. Other customers may just drop in through curiosity to see the corporate learning centre when passing by. The coordinator should not miss the opportunity to show them around and to encourage them to use the centre by pushing the need for lifelong learning for personal growth and career advancement.

While in the corporate learning centre, people should be encouraged to browse through the courseware in the display cabinets. These should be attractively laid out to grab attention and arouse interest. At the appropriate time the coordinator may point out the advantages of particular courses and name the people who have already successfully completed them. This should arouse the curiosity of the visitor who might then be encouraged to book an open learning programme.

When a client finishes a programme make them aware of other follow-up courses that might be of interest to them and bring their attention to new courses that have just arrived. This proactive approach to selling will help to keep the usage figures up. The more employees who use the corporate learning centre the more it becomes part of the life and culture of the organization.

## Mission statement

An outline of a marketing plan is shown in Figure 9.1. All good plans start with a mission statement. This sets out the purpose of the corporate learning centre and the contribution it will make to the training and development needs of the organization. The statement should be a collaborative effort between senior management, the training and development department, line managers and a representative sample of staff. It is an application of the stakeholder concept which suggests that all interested parties become involved so that they feel a sense of ownership and commitment to the centre and will thus support it. A mission statement might be worded on the following lines:

> To provide an accessible and flexible training resource which will assist local management in the achievement of business objectives by linking learning to business plans and work programmes.

## Learning centre objective

The mission statement is followed by the learning centre objectives. The objectives should be clearly stated, realistic and capable of measurement. They set down where the corporate learning centre would like to be in a few years time. They might be expressed in the form of targets of numbers of employees completing various training programmes to achieve business objectives over a defined period of time.

## Where are you now?

The next step is the position audit. Where are you now and what resources do you have?

Look at your existing situation – the hardware and course programmes you have currently in the corporate learning centre. Make a list and consider if they are the best available and meet the present and proposed needs of the centre. Ideally you should benchmark against the best of your competitors and the best currently available. It is always better to buy hardware with the more advanced specifications. Similarly, it is often false economy to buy in cheap software. It might be cheap because it is out of date or about to be superseded by a new version.

Compare this list with your objectives and you will discover the gap between your present position and your desired position.

## Marketing objectives

The marketing objectives for the corporate learning centre should be

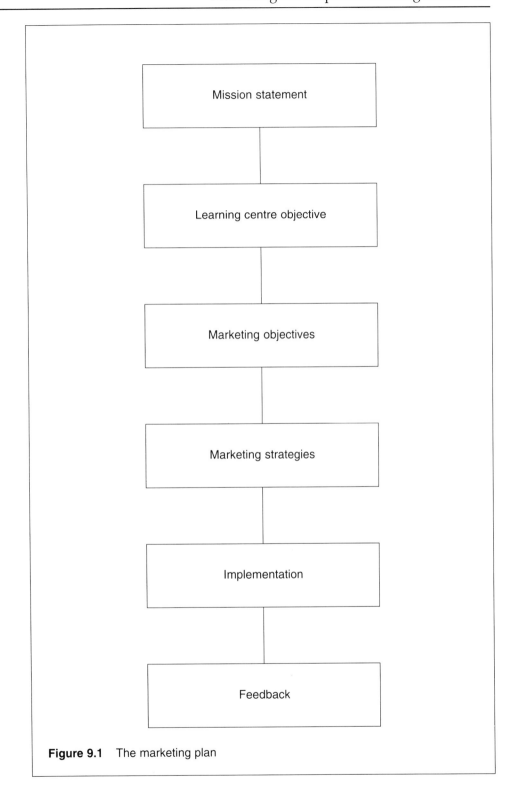

**Figure 9.1**   The marketing plan

linked to individual training plans, section work programmes, business plans and ultimately to the corporate plan. Marketing objectives can be expressed in terms of:

- persuading your existing customers to make more use of the centre
- developing new markets for your existing products
- developing new products for your existing customers
- developing new products for new markets.

In general, you should market benefits not features. Features might include types of packages, media, equipment and tutorial support. The benefits might include:

- convenience and accessibility of open learning
- development of new skills leading to more job satisfaction and prospects for promotion
- acquisition of qualifications leading to more status and better job prospects
- more productive use of free time
- self-empowerment.

## How to persuade your existing customers to make more use of the centre

There are three basic options: you may encourage learners to move on to more intensive courses, or to try new courses within the centre, or you may suggest that they use the loan service to benefit from programmes they can follow in their own time.

## Finding new customers

Your starting point for new customers should be employees within the organization who have not yet visited the centre or used the material within it. Encouraging senior and middle managers to use the centre may help promote it to all staff who will follow their lead.

Once the centre has been established you may cast your net wider to include the families of employees or staff from other organizations or contractors. The decision to extend the centre's services beyond immediate employees should be measured against the centre's mission statement and objectives and bearing in mind any security, health and safety and copyright issues it will raise.

# Club membership

Another idea might be to offer club membership of the centre with an annual subscription. Benefits of membership would include use of the centre on payment of a small fee for each course done there, a quarterly newsletter sent to subscribers and advice on sources and quality of open learning courseware. Advice on the setting up of a corporate learning centre would warrant separate negotiated fees. Club membership might help to spread the work load over the year and at the same time earn revenue for the centre.

# Consultancy

The corporate learning centre could be opened up as a training facility and consultancy service for overseas clients. Professional liability insurance may need to be taken out if you are offering a consultancy service to third parties and, once again, you should take this decision only if it accords with your mission statement and objectives and you are able to study the copyright issues.

# New products and services

The centre might offer new services such as access to the internet or stock new subjects that are currently topical and relevant to people's interests, lives and careers. Subjects of recreational interest and personal development could also be stocked. Facilities and opening hours might be improved to cater for the needs of customers. Longer opening hours might meet the needs of staff who are unable to use the services during normal working hours. Large companies may develop their own courseware which could then be sold on to other organizations.

You may identify one of the barriers to the centre's use as gaps in your course material. If potential new customers indicate a need you cannot currently fill, explore the possibility of expanding your range to attract these new customers. Once they become centre users, you may encourage them to try other existing programmes.

# New technology

Corporate learning centre courseware (and indeed hardware) quickly becomes outdated and must be replaced by more current versions. This is standard practice with computer courseware producers who update their products frequently and the coordinator should ensure that the latest version is being used.

Computer technology is moving ahead at an increasingly rapid rate. CD-ROM software is becoming more graphical and interactive and is thus taking up more computer memory space. There is an ongoing need to upgrade computer specifications in line with developments in courseware. In practice it is always better to err on the generous side when determining computer specifications as upgrading may be more expensive or, in some instances, may not be possible. Personal computers should be depreciated over two years as against four years if you wish to keep up with the best technology.

## Price and charging

The corporate learning centre will set a price for its service to meet its marketing and financial objectives. Pricing is a complex area and the system chosen will depend on the objectives of the relevant organization. The simplest pricing structure includes the addition of a mark-up to total costs, to cover any additional overheads and desired level of profits. Prices should have regard to local competition. Individual employees should not be charged for using the centre, but there may be a charge out for departments.

## Promotion

Promotion creates awareness and stimulates interest in the services of the centre. It involves advertising and techniques of publicity and personal selling. Brochures, posters, pocket diaries, pens with the corporate learning centre logo, bookmarkers, calendars, newsletters, e-mail and noticeboards are all used to advertise and keep the centre in the forefront of people's minds. Posters eventually merge into the background and lose their impact after some time, particularly if they are put on a general noticeboard and are competing with other items. Special promotions to entice employees to use the centre may occasionally be necessary. They could take the form of prizes or entry into draws for users of the centre.

Formal learning does not stop, as many people think, when you leave school or college. Marketing will remind you of this fact and encourage you to constantly upgrade your knowledge and develop new skills as the need arises. As the saying goes, 'Use it or lose it'. There is evidence to suggest that the brains of those who challenge themselves intellectually continue to grow.

## Customer database and mailing

With a personal computer, word-processing and database software the learning centre coordinator has all the resources necessary for a direct marketing campaign. The administration software will have the details on the employees who have used the centre and may also have access to the general personnel database on all employees of the company. This database can be used to target specific groups or individuals regarding new courseware or courses they have not done yet.

## Displays and brand image

A special corporate learning centre display area should be considered. Renew all posters frequently. The centre's logo should appear on screens when the computers are switched on. Stationery should also be designed. This is all part of the process of creating an identifiable brand image.

## Personal selling

Personal selling involves promoting the services of the centre to interested parties. Presentations may be designed to increase business and awareness or to create goodwill and improve the prospects of custom in the future. Personal visits to managers will help coordinators to keep in touch with training needs and demonstrate how open learning can be used to meet those needs. Actively encouraging managers to suggest new subject areas will improve commitment to the centre and usage of courses. What better way to find out what managers want than by going and asking them?

## Loan service

The coordinator must plan for the availability of the courseware and, in the case of the loan service for texts, audio and video, the distribution channel to be used. This might be the internal corporate postal system, the post office or special courier. Where there are several corporate learning centres in the company then you could consider the possibility of networking.

## Information and feedback

Once you have established your strategy, draw up an action plan to record when certain activities will take place and who exactly is responsible for them. The action plan can be converted into a budget to control expenditure. A good computer-based management information system will record course bookings and produce monthly management control information. Actual costs can be compared with budgets on a monthly basis. Actual number of bookings can be compared with targets. Market research will result in feedback from users of the centre and this should be used to improve services.

## Service – a total quality management approach (TQM)

The best form of marketing is word of mouth. Clients appreciate an excellent service, remember a good experience and will recommend the centre to their colleagues and superiors. The goodwill created will enhance and secure the centre's reputation. Total quality management means getting it right first time and should be the objective of the corporate learning centre. TQM means cost effective continuous improvement of the learning environment, the courseware and hardware resources and the quality of the service. Quality must be monitored, shortcomings identified and continuous improvement implemented. It is through TQM that the corporate learning centre will win friends and influence people.

The whole philosophy of open learning is to encourage people to learn and to go on learning throughout their careers. Any barriers that prevent them from doing this should be eliminated. Learning should be made as easy as possible. The policies of the corporate learning centre should reflect this objective. The procedures for booking courses and using the centre should be as simple as possible.

## Summary

The importance of a marketing plan was highlighted in this chapter. A systematic approach to marketing a corporate learning centre was suggested. Marketing should be thought through and not left to chance. A good plan starts with the mission statement and works through to the objectives. Marketing objectives are about retaining existing customers and creating new ones. The marketing mix strategies – a quality service, pricing, sales promotion and personal selling – will help you achieve your objectives.

# 10 The learner's guide to a corporate learning centre

## Introduction

Open learning places much of the responsibility for self-development on the learner. The corporate learning centre coordinator should use every opportunity to help and support this process. You may reproduce the material in this chapter to supply to employees. Alternatively, you may develop your own 'user guide' by drawing on the material.

## Considering the coordinator's perspective

Foresight and planning will ensure that your visit to the learning centre will have a successful outcome. Consider what you hope to learn at the course, how your manager expects you to benefit, what the course is going to be like, how to use the course, how to benefit from the course and what support systems are available in the company to help you. Support systems may include your manager, other learners, mentor, work colleagues and, of course, the coordinator.

Put yourself in the coordinator's shoes. What preparation would you like learners to have done before they visit the centre and what would you like them to do when they visit the centre? It should not need to be said, but manners and courtesy are important.

## Consulting the guide

First obtain a copy of the users' guide to courses from the coordinator. This is your map of the corporate learning centre. It will include the booking procedure, a map of where the centre is located and how to get there, and the telephone number. The guide lists all courses. However, new courses are added continuously and some may be withdrawn, so ring your coordinator to find out the up-to-date position. In the meantime, study the guide carefully. Courses may be categorized under subject area and within subject area under code, title, type – audio, video, CBT, CD-ROM and text – and duration. Remember, you may use the home loan service for audio, video and text. Armed with this information you are now in a position to discuss your needs with the learning centre co-ordinator.

## Scheduling visits

Visits to the centre will need to fit in with the demands of your work. The coordinator will try to balance your requirements against the capacity of the centre and the level of bookings. Demand will fluctuate at different times of the year, days of the week and hours of the day. Ask your coordinator when is the best time to book. The particular booth that you want may already have been booked by another person or the home loan course may have been loaned out. Remember to plan and book your requirements well in advance.

## Bookings

If booking by phone refer to the guide for the exact title of the course and its code. The length of prior notice depends on the level of demand on your learning centre, but 24 hours' notice might be considered a minimum requirement. Some facilities might be more in demand than others, for example CD-ROM based courses on information technology, and so more notice would be needed for them. Home loan courses in personal development may also be in big demand. Corporate needs such as special training initiatives may also increase the demand in specific subjects.

Remember it is good manners to let your coordinator know of cancellations well in advance, to ensure facilities are not tied up unnecessarily and other bookings can be accepted. Likewise if you change your mind regarding the course you want to do.

## Setting personal objectives

The courses in the corporate learning centre should form part of the approach to your individual training needs and your personal goals and ambitions. Individual training plans may have been drawn up by you in conjunction with your immediate supervisor or manager. There will be various ways of meeting your identified training needs, such as on-the-job and off-the-job-training. Part of your off-the-job training will be met by attending in-company and outside training programmes. Some of your formal training needs may also be met by attending corporate learning centre courses which may be more convenient and suitable for you than attending formal 'live' courses.

Your supervisor or manager should take into account the courses available in the corporate learning centre when agreeing your individual training plans. Unfortunately, this doesn't always happen. Staff attend courses outside the company at great expense even though an equivalent course is available in the local learning centre.

Setting objectives is one of the best ways of motivating yourself. Learning is a continuous process. When you have acquired one skill there are always others that could prove useful in your job and career. Nothing stands still and existing knowledge and skills need to be updated and improved from time to time. Objectives should be measurable and bounded by a time constraint – that which can be done at any time, is rarely done at all. So a time plan is most important.

Because of demands on your time and the way in which we learn, the 'little and often' approach is more effective than spending many hours at the centre in one go. With three hours devoted to open learning over the course of a week, you could acquire many skills over a period of a few months. You need persistence and commitment to be successful in open learning. Enlist the help of the coordinator when setting your objectives and drawing up your plans to achieve them. The fact that a third party knows about your plans will help you stick to your commitments.

## Choosing courses

Some courses might be of direct benefit to you in that you can apply them immediately to your work. Others might be of a developmental nature. They will contribute to your long-term development and prepare you for more demanding work or more responsible positions in the future. Self-developmental courses may help you as a person to improve your lot in life. Of course they may also indirectly benefit your working life, although this is not their prime purpose. Key and match the course to your individual – and identified – training needs. Agree the time of attendance with your immediate supervisor or manager.

Skills-based courses, such as information technology, are usually the most suitable to the corporate learning centre approach. Soft skills courses, such as interpersonal relations, public speaking and intergroup dynamics are more appropriate to a 'live' programme with participants and a course facilitator. However, the theory and knowledge content of these subjects can be learned quite effectively in a corporate learning centre. This would suggest that you use the corporate learning centre before attending these soft skills courses and that it should be formally incorporated as part of these programmes.

## Beginning with the basics

You may want to make notes while doing the course, so take a notebook and pen with you. Most courses have introductory skills sections. If you are unfamiliar with the keyboard, why not take a keyboard skills course before you tackle the more sophisticated programmes? Or a PC familiarization course? The coordinator will advise you. Remember, most of us crawl before we walk and it is a good idea to learn the fundamentals before you attempt the more difficult programmes.

## Learning outside the centre

Corporate learning centre courses are only one way of meeting your identified training needs. Other ways include on-the-job and off-the-job training. On-the-job training might include job rotation, project work, committee work and making presentations to other employees. You can, of course, use the facilities of the corporate learning centre to brush up on these areas as necessary.

Off-the-job training might include doing formal professional or certificate, diploma or degree courses. Many of the courses in the corporate learning centre will prove of benefit to your formal studies. Ask the coordinator to help you draw up a formal plan to integrate your studies with the open learning courses. You can also use the loan service and audio, video and text-based courses at home or, in the case of audio, while commuting.

## Recording your progress

The coordinator will keep a record of your attendance at corporate learning centre courses which, in turn, may form part of the personnel management information system and your personnel records. If this is the case, the coordinator will explain the system and how it works. In addition, most of the computer-based training programmes keep records of your progress during the course. As part of your individual training plans you should keep your own formal record of the courses you have attended in the corporate learning centre, including their code, description and duration. Record how you applied the course to the job and how the work situation benefited as a result. You may choose to involve your mentor or your boss in this process. The emphasis of the centre is on your learning and development and as such remains a personal issue for you.

Your record of courses attended will support any application for internal promotion. The interview panel may ask you about the courses and how you have applied them to your work situation. It is a sign of commitment to the company's goals and to your own personal development if you have a good record of attending corporate learning centre courses and it will not go unnoticed at an interview. A well maintained record of courses and their outcome and application will provide any future employer with evidence of skills and motivation.

## Using the administrator

The coordinator has a fund of knowledge about the open learning courses and will be only too delighted to share it with you, but make sure that the timing is right. There are busy days of the week and hours of the day when the coordinator may not have the time to be as helpful as he/she might wish. Use your commonsense. Ask the best time to consult about the courses and make an appropriate appointment. This will help the coordinator give you the attention you deserve. When booking your courses by phone be organized. Plan your calls in advance. Write down what you need to find out and keep the call short and to the point. Clients who haven't organized their thoughts in advance waste their own time and that of the coordinator.

## Feedback to your manager

Keep your manager informed about the courses you are doing in the corporate learning centre and it will help you to win approval. Before each course, discuss it with your manager and how it fits in with your training plan, personal development and the needs of the section. After attending the course discuss the benefits of the programme with the manager and how the work of the section is going to improve as a result of your application. Continuous feedback with your manager will reinforce the benefits of your learning and development and provide you with help and advice in return.

## Feedback to your coordinator

The coordinator will help you choose the most appropriate course and identify other training suitable to your needs when you are ready to pursue more advanced courses or different programmes. If you consult your coordinator when you are about to attend an external course, he/she may be able to suggest a precourse familiarizer which will help you learn more effectively on the 'live' programme. Learning centre courses may also be used to revise and reinforce knowledge and skills acquired on 'live' courses. Your feedback and suggestions will help the coordinator to develop the centre's service and identify and purchase new courses.

## Personal housekeeping

At the centre keep your work area tidy. When you are finished put your courseware away in the presses or give it back to the coordinator. Return the screen to the menu ready for the next learner. Remove your personal belongings. A little thought will help the coordinator and other learners. Remember the next learner is your internal customer – so leave the booth in the condition you would like to have it for yourself. Fill out any course evaluation forms and hand them to the coordinator before you leave. If you want to book in for more sessions during the rest of the week now might be a good opportunity to do so.

## Summary

Preparation is the key to success. Getting the most from your corporate learning centre means planning and thinking ahead. Make the most of your visit by paying attention to the following points:

- schedule your visits having regard to the exigencies of the work situation and the demands on the learning centre
- book your course requirements in advance
- set yourself objectives and draw up a timeplan
- choose courses in line with your individual training plan and agree them with your manager
- use the centre as part of your overall training and development plan
- keep a record of completed courses
- use the coordinator's experience to your advantage
- inform your manager about your plans and progress
- inform your coordinator about all your training plans
- keep your work area tidy while at the centre.

# 11 Conclusions and recommendations

## 24 Questions for planning a centre

1   What is the likely market for your centre?

2   What topics will it cover?

3   What types of courseware should it contain?

4   How and where will you source courseware?

5   What sort of media should it have?

6   Where will it be located?

7   How should it be equipped, furnished and laid out?

8   Who are the suppliers of equipment?

9   What is the timetable for set up?

10   What are the centre's mission and objectives?

11   What are the forces which help and hinder the corporate learning centre?

12   How will it integrate with 'live' training programmes?

13   What will be the staffing arrangements?

14   How much support will the company give staff to use open learning?

15   What training will the coordinator require?

16   What size of budget will be needed for setting up and running the centre?

17   In the case of multisites, should they be stand alone or networked?

18   Will the centre be treated as a profit centre or absorbed as an overhead?

19   How will you identify training needs?

20   How will you evaluate courseware?

21   How will you advertise and promote the centre?

22   How will you attract new customers to the centre in the short, medium and long term?

23   How will you monitor the operation of the centre and establish whether or not it is a success?

24   How will you operate the stock and loans management system for audio, video and text-based courses?

# The future

The accessibility, flexibility and convenience of corporate learning centres should ensure a bright future in meeting identified training and development needs. The sense of isolation and lack of social interaction will mean they will never completely replace traditional training but will complement and enrich it.

In 1993 a European Commission survey estimated that by the year 2000 over 90 per cent of all workers in Europe will use a PC or computer terminal. This raises the possibility of Just in Time Training (JITT) where employees could access training courseware as and when they need it. The technology is already available. Using a local area network (LAN), PCs in the same building can be linked together. PCs which are distributed over wider geographical areas can be linked together using a national or an international wide area network (WAN). Training can now be delivered direct to the learner's own PC.

The television set will be important in the learning centre of the future. With cable link the technology is already in place. Subscription learning channels could incorporate a menu for users to integrate a course programme of their choice. With developments in technology the PC can also double as a TV. There are already PCs on sale which can do this. The future penetration of the domestic market with PCs/TVs means that there is the nucleus of a corporate learning centre in each household. The technology is there. It is now a question of creating the demand for the service.

# Continuous marketing

To maintain interest and a high rate of usage in a corporate learning centre, continuous marketing is necessary. Existing packages must be updated and new programmes purchased. These must be vetted carefully by subject experts for relevance and quality. Nothing does more damage to a corporate learning centre's image than poor quality courses. To attract custom, self-developmental and recreational packages should also be stocked. Marketing research using a questionnaire is needed on an annual or more frequent basis to keep in touch with the views and needs of the centre's users.

# Management support

A corporate learning centre cannot be successful without the active support of top management, from the chief executive down. Senior managers, as role models and as an expression of their active support and commitment, should use the centre themselves, if only on an occasional basis. If the chief executive were to use the centre even infrequently it would work wonders for bookings. Leadership should be by example. Attendance at corporate learning centre courses should be an issue at interviews for internal positions. If word gets around that it helps career progression, ambitious people will be very eager to do open learning courses.

Managers should actively encourage their staff to use the corporate learning centre to meet individual training needs and for personal development. Open learning should be incorporated into the culture of the company. Allowance for centre usage should be an integral part of work programmes, individual training plans and budgets. Usage should be reviewed by managers each month.

Managers should allocate at least two hours official time to each staff member for this purpose. In practice some staff complain that they are unable to do corporate learning centre courses because of pressure of work and that managers do not encourage them to use its services. For job-related courses as much time as is practicable should be allowed. If an employee needs 20 hours for a particular course then the manager should schedule this over a number of weeks.

# Outside working hours

The take-up of courses in the corporate learning centre outside normal working hours is usually sporadic. This is understandable since people have other lives to lead outside their work. Some type of monetary incentive may be necessary to improve usage outside of working hours. Staff might be encouraged to use the twilight hours between 4pm and 7pm immediately after work. This saves them the trouble of going home and coming back again. Weekends may also be targeted.

## Organizational databases

In the future greater use will be made of information technology to provide facilities for learning and information on the design of in-house customized courses. Dorrell (1993) supports this view. She reckons organizations will have databases with information on:

company background

organization charts, where necessary

company culture and mission statements

departmental/divisional responsibilities

individual responsibilities and how these relate to each other, and

whole organization job descriptions.

Most large organizations already have this information on file. These courses could be designed using a variety of media including print, audio, video, CBT and CD-ROM. Thus induction courses could be run in the corporate learning centre. New employees can help themselves to this information as needed and assimilate it quicker and more effectively.

## Corporate learning centre management

The success or failure of a corporate learning centre depends very much on the calibre, commitment and dedication of the coordinator and local management. The enthusiasm of line management and staff is also a prerequisite. The coordinator must have excellent customer relations and information technology skills, while the manager needs to have a special interest in educational technology, marketing and learning and the training and development of staff.

Functionally, the corporate learning centres could be part of training and development or under the control of the local personnel manager or line manager. If the company has a corporate library, this might be the best place to site the centre as it is a complementary service. However, its location and management will depend on the particular culture and circumstances of the company. In a large multisite organization, corporate learning centres should be networked rather than stand-alone entities.

# Summary

Over the next few years corporate learning centres will play a prominent role in the delivery of quality training programmes within companies. To be successful five basic criteria must be met:

1   Appropriate hardware and accommodation resources must be provided.
2   A wide range of quality courseware must be stocked.
3   The centre must be staffed by a capable full-time coordinator.
4   The centre must be supported by management and staff.
5   The centre must be actively marketed.

# Appendix I

# A case study of corporate learning centres at Sun Life

This case study is presented with the permission of John Wyatt, Training and Development Consultant, Sun Life. He describes the introduction of a corporate learning centre into Sun Life. It originally appeared as a special report in *Money Marketing* in July 1995 and in *Financial Training Review*, August 1994.

John Wyatt has the optimistic air of someone participating in a new and promising business project. Sun Life ventured into the world of multimedia at the beginning of 1994 when it opened a corporate learning centre at its Bristol office, and so far the response has been encouraging, both in terms of numbers of people using the centre and what they had to say about it.

Not bad for a company which four years earlier had only two or three PCs in most departments. What's more, the corporate learning centre has been so successful that the company is considering further centres in London and in each of the other four offices in Bristol. It is also piloting the use of CD-ROM training systems within its nationwide branch network.

The corporate learning centre holds books, audiotapes, videos, computer-based training packages and multimedia training programmes. No internal charge is made for using these resources and they are very popular with all departments within the company.

## Launching the corporate learning centre

In January 1994 managers and training staff were invited to view the courses now available at the corporate learning centre. Sixty people

107

attended and took away an information pack which included a one-page synopsis of all the courses and details of how to book. John says: 'We had two fears, that the idea would be incredibly popular and we would not be able to cope or that no one would come'. In the event, neither was justified. From an initial level of 15 training sessions during February the figure has risen to between 50 and 80 sessions per month.

## Benefits of open learning

As a means of training, open learning is very flexible. It enables a large number of users to be trained on the same material and it overcomes one of the main problems of face-to-face training: namely, that staff sometimes need immediate training on a given subject but the next face-to-face training course may not be scheduled for another three weeks, or even longer in the case of external courses. With corporate learning, users can decide the time and date of their training and they can also choose how long they want to study. They simply book into the centre in much the same way that they would book themselves on to a face-to-face training course.

The corporate learning centre is the culmination of what has been a fairly typical technology-based training evolution. The company started by buying in computer-based training packages, then began to develop its own. Eventually, it bought an interactive video workstation – a laserdisk player and PC, with a DVA 4000 card – and then a series of multimedia PCs capable of running CD-ROM programmes.

## Introduction of CD-ROM

Sun Life signed a two-year contract for IIS interactive video courses, which also gave access to Longman's programmes. The outcome was a 12-module revolving library with training credits for short-term training needs. There are five interactive video titles. However, these have been overshadowed by the CD-ROM programmes which have attracted the most interest. CD-ROM stands for compact disk read-only memory. It is an extension of CD audio, which stores moving video, text and graphics as sound on a compact disk.

With CD-ROM, the cost of the hardware is low compared with other technologies such as interactive video. This low cost combined with CD-ROM's ease of use and standardization makes it an attractive investment.

The CD-ROM training programmes have proved very popular with trainers and trainees. In typical formats, users are shown lively scenarios and they interact a mouse to stop the action, answer questions, skip over details or delve deeper into particular subjects, choose alternative responses or receive constructive feedback on the implications of their choices. If there is anything they have not completely understood on any given point, they can go back over it as many times as necessary.

To move around the CD-ROM training programmes and review different sections, a user simply moves the cursor around the screen and selects options by clicking a button. Trainers can also show images from the interactive sections on a monitor to a bigger audience to stimulate group discussion.

## CD-ROM training programmes

The company's introduction to CD-ROM training programmes came at Multimedia '93, when John Wyatt saw two programmes from Xebec Multi Medial Solutions. The programmes were comprehensive, easy to use and the graphic quality and the level of interaction were excellent. Both of them were bought. These programmes were shown to a number of training customer service departments, who felt that the training was consistent with that delivered at their stand-up courses and they also liked the humour in the programmes.

It was felt that the time was right to invest in CD-ROM because they were confident that the technology had developed to such an extent that it would not become obsolete overnight. So far, this investment is paying dividends. Users have expressed 80–90 per cent satisfaction with the multimedia method. Most important, any initial resistance from the trainers themselves has been overcome. They now see multimedia as a way of enhancing their skills rather than replacing them.

They now have a number of CD-ROM training programmes, including Xebec's programmes: Business Calls (for telephone skills); Leading Teams (leadership skills); Business Words (writing skills); Managing Tasks and Activities (organization skills); Business Communications (interpersonal skills); Business Meetings; Money Business 1 (cash flow) and Money Business 2 (budgets). One advantage of the Xebec programmes is that they all have a consistent format and layout, which reduces the time it takes for a user to become familiar with how each programme works and how to move around it.

## Basic skills programmes

Business Calls and Business Words are two programmes which are extremely useful. They overcome the embarrassment factor that people may have felt about signing up for a face-to-face course on what might be thought of as basic skills. With these programmes users are free to ask questions and they can experiment freely in the simulation exercises without fear of real-life consequences. They have helped to improve the standard of writing skills and telephone technique across the company, to the delight of the customer service departments.

The workbooks which come with each of the Xebec programmes have also proved popular. They really are genuine workbooks, which are photocopied so that each user can keep his or her own copy. They have been tailored to the company's own needs by adding its own front cover on to each book so that they convey a consistent identity with their other working manuals. They are now looking to expand their range of multimedia programmes to include IT and software training as well as financial programmes.

## Support

Support for the corporate learning centre has been very simple. There is a booking system (people can choose when they want to come between 9am and 5pm on weekdays) and the trainers and training administrative staff are located near to the room housing the computers. They can thus greet students and show people how to operate the system. John says: 'There has not been a need for a member of training staff dedicated to supporting the centre. The few problems with the hardware and software have been easily solved. The technology is performing well.'

## Complements face-to-face training

Although Sun Life is committed to open learning, it has not replaced face-to-face training. Open learning enables users to study without direct supervision and this gives trainers more time to carry out a coaching and mentoring role. This is important because trainees at all levels must have a facilitator or mentor to provide information and encouragement.

It is now looking to see how it can integrate open learning sections into its stand-up training programmes. Open learning could teach the theory before the practice, effectively cutting a two-day course into a single-day workshop. People like to learn in different ways and they are simply catering for all tastes. However, it does appear that the future of training at Sun Life will see more and more revolving five-inch disks.

# Appendix II

# Information sources

1 Other corporate learning centres

2 *The Open Learning Directory* lists a wide range of materials and is available from Heineman Publishers Oxford, Customer Services Department, PO Box 283, Oxon OX2 8RU. Tel: 01865 310366

3 British Association for Open Learning, Suite no 16, Pixmoor House, Pixmoor Avenue, Letchworth, Herts SG6 1JG. Tel: 01462 485588

4 Training managers in other companies. Consult the IPD register for members.

# Bibliography

Austin, Mary B. 1992. 'CBT From Scratch – Building a computer based training department. *Tech Trends*, vol. 37, pp. 9–11.

Bajtelmit, John W. 1990. 'Study methods in distance education: a summary of five research studies', *Contemporary Issues in American Distance Education*, ed. Michael G. Moore, Pergamon Press, Oxford, pp. 181–91.

Bates, Tony. 1988. 'Delivery and new technology', *Open Learning in Transition: An Agenda for Action*, ed. Nigel Paine, National Extension College, Cambridge, pp. 364–77.

Birchall, D. 1990. 'Third generation distance learning', *Journal of European Industrial Training*, vol. 14, 7, pp. 17–20.

Boulding, T. 1989. 'Long-distance learning', *Personnel Management*, vol. 21, 1, pp. 31–2.

Chute, Alan G., Balthazar, Lee B., Poston, Carol O. 1990. 'Learning from teletraining: what AT & T research says', *Contemporary Issues in American Education*, ed. Michael G. Moore, Pergamon Press, Oxford, pp. 260–75.

Coldeway, Dan O. 1982. 'What does educational psychology tell us about the adult learner at a distance?', *Learning at a Distance: A World Perspective*, eds John S. Daniel, Martha A. Stroud, John R. Thompson, Athabasca University/International Correspondence Education, Edmonton, pp. 90–3.

Crawley, Richard. 1988. 'Flexible training systems: breaking the mould of training in Britain', *Open Learning in Transition: An Agenda for Action*, ed. Nigel Paine, National Extension College, Cambridge, pp. 326–36.

Daniel, John. 1988. 'The worlds of open learning', *Open Learning in Transition: An Agenda for Action*, ed. Nigel Paine, National Extension College, Cambridge, pp. 126–36.

113

Davies, W.J.K. 1989. *Open And Flexible Learning Centres*, National College for Educational Technology, London.

Dobson, Roger. 1988. 'Tomorrow's training today', *Open Learning in Transition: An Agenda for Action*, ed. Nigel Paine, National Extension College, Cambridge, pp. 319–25.

Dorrell, Julia. 1993. *Resource-Based Learning. Using Open and Flexible Learning Resources for Continuous Development*, McGraw-Hill Training Series, London.

Draper, James A. 1982. 'Adult education: a perspective for the eighties', *Learning at a Distance: A World Perspective*, eds John S. Daniel, Martha A. Stroud and John R. Thompson, Athabasca University/International Council for Correspondence Education, Edmonton, pp. 43–6.

Dryden, Gordon and Vos, Jeannette. 1994. *The Learning Revolution*, Accelerated Learning Systems, p. 43.

Dwyer, Frank M. 1990. 'Enhancing the effectiveness of distance education: a proposed research agenda', *Contemporary Issues in American Distance Education*, ed. Michael G. Moore, Pergamon Press, Oxford, pp. 221–9.

Fahy, Michael. 1989. 'Long distance learning', *Network Work*, vol. 6, 48, pp. 39–40.

Ferrar, Phil. 1991. 'Opening learning for business success at Bradford & Bingley', *International Journal of Bank Marketing*, vol. 9, 4, pp. 17–9.

Florina, Barbara M. 1990. 'Delivery systems for distance education: focus on computer conferencing', *Contemporary Issues in American Education*, ed. Michael G. Moore, Pergamon Press, Oxford, pp. 277–89.

Forlenza, D. May 1995. 'Computer-based training', *Professional Safety*, vol. 40, 5, pp. 28–9.

Forsythe, Kathleen. 1982. 'Learning to learn', *Learning at a Distance: A World Perspective*, ed. John S. Daniel, Martha A. Stroud, John R. Thompson, Athabasca University/International Council for Correspondence Education, Edmonton, pp. 219–21.

Fox, Bruce. December 1994. 'Dominick's employees train with multimedia computers', *Chain Store Age Executive*, pp. 71–2.

Franchi, Jorge. 1992. 'CBT or IVD? – that's the question', *Tech Trends*, vol. 37, 2, pp. 27–30.

Freathy, Paul. 1991. 'Distance learning and the distributive trades: Stirling's MBA', *Journal of European Industrial Training*, vol. 15, 4, pp. 21–4.

Freeman, Richard. 1982. 'Flexistudy', *Learning at a Distance: A World Perspective*, eds John S. Daniel, Martha A. Stroud, John R. Thompson, Athabasca University/International Council for Correspondence Education, Edmonton, pp. 162–5.

Fricker, John. 1988. 'Open learning – what's in it for business?', *Open Learning in Transition: An Agenda for Action*, ed. Nigel Paine, National Extension College, Cambridge, pp. 337–47.

Fuller, Alison and Murray, Saunders. 1990. 'The paradox in open learning at work', *Personnel Review*, vol. 19, 5, pp. 29–33.

Ganger, Ralph E. November 1994. 'Training: computer-based', *Personnel*

*Journal*, pp. 1–5.

Gibson, Chere Campell. 1990. 'Learners and learning: a discussion of selected research', *Contemporary Issues in American Distance Education*, ed. Michael G. Moore, Pergamon Press, Oxford, pp. 121–33.

Handy, Charles. 1988. 'The new management', *Open Learning In Transition: An Agenda for Action*, ed. Nigel Paine, National Extension College, Cambridge, pp. 116–25.

Harper, Karl. 1993. 'Why flexible learning?' *Banking World*, vol. 11, 8, pp. 45–6.

Johnston, Rita. 1993. 'The role of distance learning in professional development', *Management Services,* vol 37, 4, pp. 24–6.

Kattackal, R. December, 1994. 'Plugging in to computer based training', *Internal Auditor,* vol 51, 6, pp. 32–6.

Kay, Alan S. June 1995. 'The business case for multi-media', *Datamation*, vol. 41, 11, pp. 55–6.

Keegan, Desmond. 1990. *Foundations of Distance Education*, 2nd ed., Routledge, London and New York, pp. 3–45 and 183–209.

Lavitt, Michael O. January 1995. 'Multimedia system provides training in aircraft ID', *Aviation Week and Space Technology*, vol. 142, 2, p. 54.

Lewis, Roger. 1988. 'Open learning – the future', *Open Learning in Transition: An Agenda for Action*, ed. Nigel Paine, National Extension College, Cambridge, pp. 175–89.

Linstead, Stephen. 1990. 'Developing management meta-competence: can distance learning help?' *Journal of European Industrial Training,* vol. 14, 6, pp. 17–27.

Littlefield, David. September 1994. 'Open learning by PC or paper?' *Personnel Management*, vol. 26, 9, p. 55.

Lougher, John. 1988. 'High-tech training in British Steel', *Open Learning in Transition: An Agenda for Action*, ed. Nigel Paine, National Extension College, Cambridge, pp. 379–98.

Markowitz, Jr. Harold. 1990. 'Continuing professional development in distance education', *Contemporary Issues in American Distance Education*, ed. Michael G. Moore, Pergamon Press, Oxford, pp. 58–66.

Marx, W. February 1995. 'The new high tech training', *Management Review*, vol. 84, 2, pp. 57–60.

Murray, P. January 1993. 'Quality learning, a personal view, from a fan of open learning', *BACIE,* vol. 93, 1, pp. 8–9.

Oates, David. 1990. 'Small business: switched on to distance learning', *Director*, vol. 43, 12, p. 127.

Richardson, Michael. 1988. 'The National Extension College and the Open University – a comparison of two national institutions', *Open Learning In Transition: An Agenda for Action*, ed. Nigel Paine, National Extension College, Cambridge, pp. 57–69.

Shlechter, T.M. 1990. 'The relative instructional efficiency of small group computer based training', *Journal of Educational Computing Research*, vol. 6, 3, pp. 329–41.

Stephenson, Stanley D. August 1992. 'The role of the instructor in computer-based training', *Performance & Instruction*, vol. 31, 7, pp. 23–6.

Temple, Hilary. 1988. 'Open learning in a changing climate', *Open Learning In Transition: An Agenda for Action*, ed. Nigel Paine, National Extension College, Cambridge, pp. 201–11.

Thorpe, Mary. 1993. *Evaluating Open and Distance Learning*, Longman, Harlow.

Tuckett, Alan. 1988. 'Open learning and the education of adults', *Open Learning in Transition: An Agenda for Action*, ed. Nigel Paine, National Extension College, Cambridge, pp. 156–71.

Van den Brande, Lieve. 1993. *Flexible and Distance Learning*, John Wiley & Sons, New York, pp. 1–34 and 233–8.

Waniewiczz, Ignacy. 1982. 'The adult learners: who are they, why and where do they learn?' *Learning at a Distance: A World Perspective*, eds John S. Daniel, Martha A. Stroud, John R. Thompson, Athabasca University/International Council for Correspondence Education, Edmonton, pp. 87–9.

Waterhouse, Philip. 1990. *Flexible Learning*, Network Educational Press, Bath.

Wedemeyer, Charles A. 1981. *Learning at the Back Door*, The University of Wisconsin Press, Wisconsin and London, pp. 47–73.

Williams, Shirley. 1988. 'Education and the information revolution', *Open Learning in Transition: An Agenda for Action*, ed. Nigel Paine, National Extension College, Cambridge, pp. 81–91.

# Index

# Analysing Learning Needs

Malcolm Craig

The way we work is changing dramatically: shouldn't the way we analyse training needs be changing too? That question lies at the heart of Dr Craig's thought-provoking book. He examines new working patterns, changes in the relationships between skills, the wholesale shift from motor to cognitive skills and the increasing use of part-time workers. Against this background he sets out a holistic approach to what he calls, significantly, "learning needs".

According to Dr Craig, the traditional techniques are no longer adequate. Instead he offers a range of "investigative" methods designed to identify learning needs and determine what kinds of support would be appropriate. After explaining each method he gives examples and case studies showing how it can be applied. In addition there are numerous self-diagnosis sections to encourage readers to relate the ideas and techniques to their own situation. The result is a book that will enable managers and specialists alike to improve the effectiveness of training in their organization dramatically.

1994          160 pages          0 566 07448 6

# Gower

# Gower Handbook of Training and Development

## 2nd Edition

Edited by John Prior, MBE

This Gower Handbook, published in association with the Institute of Training and Development, first appeared in 1991 and quickly established itself as a standard work. For this new edition the text has been completely revised to reflect recent developments and new chapters have been added on cultural diversity, learning styles and choosing resources. The *Handbook* now contains contributions from no fewer than forty-nine experienced professionals, each one an expert in his or her chosen subject.

For anyone involved in training and development, whether in business or the public sector, the *Handbook* represents an unrivalled resource.

1994          640 pages          0 566 07446 X

Gower

# Guide to In-Company Training Methods

Leslie Rae

Learning at the workplace is usually the cheapest way to train - it is often the best. Leslie Rae's book covers the processes and the skills involved in training without incurring the expense of sending people on external courses. The methods he describes range from 'sitting next to Nellie' through delegation, coaching, mentoring, team development and self-development to one-to-one instruction. He explains in detail the structures and techniques required and provides checklists, formats and guidelines to supplement the text.

Both line managers and professional trainers will profit from a study of this important new book by one of the UK's best known training experts.

1992          190 pages          0 566 07297 1

Gower

# A Handbook for Training Strategy

Martyn Sloman

The traditional approach to training in the organization is no longer effective. That is the central theme of Martyn Sloman's challenging book. A new model is required that will reflect the complexity of organizational life, changes in the HR function and the need to involve line management. This *Handbook* introduces such a model and describes the practical implications not only for human resource professionals and training managers but also for line managers.

Martyn Sloman writes as an experienced training manager and his book is concerned above all with implementation. Thus his text is supported by numerous questionnaires, survey instruments and specimen documents. It also contains the findings of an illuminating survey of best training practice carried out among UK National Training Award winners.

The book is destined to make a significant impact on the current debate about how to improve organizational performance. With its thought-provoking argument and practical guidance it will be welcomed by everyone with an interest in the business of training and development.

1994          240 pages          0 566 07393 5

Gower

# Handbook of Management Games

## 5th Edition

Chris Elgood

This is the fifth edition of what is, quite simply, the most comprehensive reference to management games available, covering everything from how to run them to how to obtain them. The book explains what management games are, how the types differ from each other and how they compare with other methods of promoting learning. It offers a rationale for their use and confronts the difficulties of nomenclature that exist and the relationship between different views of the learning process. Also examined is the relationship between enjoyment and learning.

The directory section has descriptions of about 300 currently available management games, classified in various ways. Administrative details such as the number of players, the number of teams and the time required are provided, together with information on target group, subject areas, nature and purpose.

1993          352 pages          0 566 07306 4

# Gower

# How to Write a Training Manual

John Davis

Course documentation is a subject largely ignored in trainer education. Yet it is central to success in the training room. A well-thought-out training manual • ensures high-quality presentation first time and every time a course is run • promotes better course management and more professional delivery • facilitates the review and, where necessary, the modification of training material • leads to the correct balance between creativity, flexibility and professional discipline.

John Davis' book - the first of its kind - shows how to prepare documentation using a format designed to clarify content, timing, delivery, pace and style. Drawing on his own extensive experience, he offers practical guidelines supported throughout by detailed examples. For trainers and training managers seeking to improve their performance, his advice is not to be missed.

1992          144 pages          0 566 07325 0

Gower

# Running an Effective Training Session

## Patrick Forsyth

This down-to-earth guide to planning and delivering a training session will be welcomed by new and experienced trainers alike - as well as by line managers and other professionals with training responsibility. In this book Patrick Forsyth takes the reader step by step through the process of structuring the session and preparing materials, before covering the presentational techniques involved in detail. The final section is concerned with following up in terms of evaluation and establishing links to further training. The user-friendly text is supported throughout by examples.

For anyone involved in training, Patrick Forsyth's book represents a painless way to improve performance.

1992     144 pages     Hardback   0 566 07320 X     Paperback   0 566 07619 5

Gower

# 35 Checklists for Human Resource Management

Ian MacKay

The late Ian MacKay started producing his checklists in the early years of his work as a lecturer in human resource management. They reflected his view that the role of the lecturer is not so much to teach as to help others to learn and, above all, to think for themselves.

From 1985 onwards, Ian MacKay's checklists were a regular - and outstandingly popular - feature of the Institute of Training and Development's journal. A collection in book form, *35 Checklists for Human Resource Development*, was published in 1989 and has found an appreciative, and steadily growing, readership. This companion volume covers a wide variety of human resource issues, from apparently mundane tasks like designing application forms to issues of the utmost sensitivity like appraisal, grievance-handling and redundancy policy.

As in the previous volume, the checklists are not designed to provide easy answers. What they will do is help you to think in a structured way about your attitudes and behaviour. Your responses can then become a basis for increasing your effectiveness. Personnel specialists, and others involved in human resource management, will find working through the checklists a challenging and rewarding exercise.

1993          184 pages          0 566 07433 8

Gower

# Training Evaluation Handbook

A C Newby

Based on the author's highly successful Training Evaluation Audit Method (TEAM), this book will help trainers in any kind of organization to develop more effective programmes. The first part of the book examines the strategic role of training evaluation and discusses some of the political issues involved. Part II presents a range of techniques for improving training effectiveness, and shows how to develop instruments that both assess and reinforce learning. In the final part a series of case studies shows how the author's methods have been used in a wide variety of businesses and functions.

If what you are looking for is a systematic way of reviewing and strengthening the training provision in your own organization, then *Training Evaluation Handbook* is for you.

| 1992 | 324 pages | 0 566 02837 9 |

# Gower